EVIL IN GOD'S GOOD HANDS

ENOCH DEBOSS

dew
mercies
PUBLISHING

Copyright © 2024 by Enoch Deboss
All rights reserved.

Cover design by Enoch Deboss
Cover copyright © 2024 by Enoch Deboss

Dew Mercies Publishing supports the right to and the value of copyright. Any scanning, uploading, and distribution of this book without permission is a theft of the author's intellectual property.

No part of this book may be reproduced in any form on or by an electronic or mechanical means, including information storage and retrieval systems, without permission in writing from the publisher, except by a reviewer who may quote brief passages in a review.

The contents of this book represent the beliefs of the author. Any attempt to misconstrue the intent of the author's words will be disregarded. Any attempt to take the author's words out of the author's intended context will be disregarded.

This book is an expression of the author's right to free speech, and all authorial intent is not derived from the reader's interpretation, but all authorial intent belongs to the author, and will be derived from the interpretations of the author.

Dew Mercies Publishing is not responsible for websites (or their content) that are not owned by the aforementioned publisher.

First Edition: December 2024

ISBN-13:
978-1-7382832-0-0 (trade paperback)
978-1-7382832-1-7 (hardcover)
978-1-7382832-2-4 (ebook)

Dew Mercies Publishing

TABLE OF CONTENTS

FOREWORD
THE GOSPEL OF JESUS CHRIST ... i

CHAPTER 1
God Created Evil - Blasphemy? ... 1

CHAPTER 2
Three Good Doctrines You Need For Evil (Part 1) ... 13

CHAPTER 3
Three Good Doctrines You Need For Evil (Part 2) ... 69

CHAPTER 4
God Created Evil - A Biblical Argument ... 115

CHAPTER 5
Is God Evil? Is God An Evildoer? ... 159

TABLE OF CONTENTS

CHAPTER 6
Evil Is In God's Good Hands ... 171

EPILOGUE
The Stress Test For Sound Doctrine ... 209

BIBLIOGRAPHY ... 224

Dark providences, never understood before, will then be clearly seen, and all that puzzles us now will become plain to us in the light of the Lamb.

CHARLES H. SPURGEON

FOREWORD
The Gospel of Jesus Christ

ABOVE all, I hold fast to this doctrine: When I observe how creation speaks, her order and function declare the existence of a God, but the Bible, bound and sealed, unfolds the character of the True and Living God on its pages.

Preserved throughout the ages, it is in this book we are faced with the undeniable — God has created all things. Be it in heaven or on earth, be it seen or unseen, God has said that He has done it. With one verse, the universe is established, and in six days the heavens and earth are completed. God sets His face to all that He has made, He knows its purpose, and He calls it good.

Man can trace his heritage to the very beginning, and learn his place within God's beautiful design. Mankind, male and female, were made by God to bear His image and likeness. Formed out of dust and breath, we visibly reflect the excellencies of the invisible God.

Our parents, Adam and Eve, embodied these perfections for a time, as God gave them authority to fill and rule the earth. As a loving Father, God gave them a place to meet with Him, a work to occupy their days, and commands to order their steps and preserve their peace. They were given everything. Sadly, for Adam and Eve, everything was not enough. In their pursuit for more, they aligned their ambition with Satan, an adversary who promised them everything they already had at the cost of their obedience. To pursue forbidden fruit was a fruitless endeavour, and our first parents' rebellion introduced sin and death into the world.

You may ask, what *is* sin? In its simplest form, sin is when man does not obey God's commands. Yet, guised in simplicity, sin has shaped our reality, and has warped our very existence. Will we deny the power of sin? Reader, will you deny what you know and see?

For sin has changed our relationship with God. We are no longer children of glory, but criminals of wrath. God will not reward disobedience with life, but will rightly punish disobedience with death. To violate His loving commands is an offence of the highest order.

We owe our Creator a debt we cannot truly pay, and God's wrath sits over our heads like a guillotine, waiting to drop in a moment we know not, to collect payment for our crimes. All men fear the day death will take us from this life, bring us before His court, and we are pronounced "Guilty!" and escorted to hell's fire. Man is not at peace with God.

Sin has hardened our way with creation. Long ago, the earth opened her hands, and nature freely yielded its bounty. But with sin's corruption, we are tasked to toil, and attempt to bring good fruit from cursed grounds. Death strikes every end of the physical universe, and the earth says she is stricken with death, decay, sickness and calamity. If the fire does not consume us, the tsunami may swallow us up. If we escape the fire and storm, the hurricane may uproot and sweep us away in its violent winds. And if we escape all these, the earthquake may shake our very foundations, and turn the most fortified city to dust. Calamity and destruction sit upon the face of the earth, and when creation lashes out, we are at its mercy. All is not right with the world.

Sin has perverted our relationship with each other. Is sin not more apparent than how we treat our neighbour? From the very beginning, man has fanned sin's embers into flames to set the world on fire. The dignity and value God attaches to every human life is far removed from our hearts and minds, as sin causes us to exalt ourselves, while diminishing the well-being and interests of others. Pride, hatred, murder, wars, racism, slavery, envy, lust, rape, adultery, sexual deviances, idolatry, greed, stealing and deceit defile human history because of an evil we all share within. Humanity has grown cold in loving their neighbour.

What is around us is a reflection of what is *in* us. Broken and corrupt societies are built by broken and corrupt men. Sin first took root in the human heart with Adam and Eve, and as a child physically inherits the image of their parents, all of us have spiritually inherited sin from our forefathers. From above, we are not right with God, but within, we are just not right.

There is no harmony. Heart, body, mind, soul and spirit — all of which make a man — is disturbed and darkened by sin. It is a plague, and no remedy of our making can free us of this disease. The Bible exposes the depths of our sin-sickness with an inconvenient truth: We *love* our sin. It threatens our welfare in this life and the next, but as an alluring addiction, we love clinging to what enslaves us. It is in our very nature.

Reader, do you *know* that you are a sinner? Do you know you are acquainted with much evil and darkness? Every evil desire, thought and act, every violation of God's commands is evidence of your allegiance to the sin in you. Lovers of sin are enemies of God, and those loyal to sin are rewarded with death.

And what is death? Death is not only to die, but to be forever separated from the One who is and holds true life. Do not let your daily living deceive you. Being alive does not mean you actually are. To be separated from True Life makes the most animate and lively man as dead bones, a carcass that will only know decay and destruction in the end. Our time in the grave tells us much about our present condition while we live. Beyond the grave, hell awaits and those who were always dead will know they were *truly* dead all along. In these ways, sin and death have partnered together, and lay hold on our once-perfect world. As a result, all of us are in a predicament most miserable.

Under the weight of this reality, two words ring out in my soul: *But God!* We ought to be pitied and helpless, but God did not leave us in despair. The God who is set to uphold holiness and justice graciously offers mercy to those who have fallen. We have reason to rejoice in despair, for in the Bible, God proclaimed that He would send Someone who would save men from their sins.

At the appointed time, God gives of Himself and sends the Son, who is God, into our world to deliver salvation and freedom. God the Son entered into human history as a man, miraculously born of a virgin woman, and is given the name Jesus Christ. Fully God yet fully man, Christ would dwell among and walk beside us, but Christ's departure from heaven to earth is not simply to be *with* us — Jesus came to suffer and die for sinners.

Why must Christ die? That is the only way our salvation is realized. When we observe the pattern of the natural world, we know day and night never cease. Day gives way to night, and night gives way to day. It is a cycle as old as time. The seasons are ordered in a similar manner. Each season has their place, but they change hands, as spring turns into summer, and fall turns into winter to meet spring again. The earth is bound by these cycles, for God has commanded it to be so. They are natural laws which govern the natural world.

But the world is not only governed by natural laws, for in His wisdom, God has also issued laws to govern the realm of the unseen. From the beginning, there have been spiritual laws in place, though we cannot physically observe them through creation. Thank God for His Bible, where His spiritual laws are made plain in ink!

So why must Christ die? Because God's spiritual law is this: Without the shedding of blood, there is no forgiveness of sins. The God of heaven is willing to offer forgiveness to sinners, He is willing to acquit guilty men of their crimes, but it comes at a price. Blood must be shed, life must be laid down if the eternal punishment for sin is to be lifted from our heads. Men like you and I can do nothing, for no sinful man can set this law in motion; God requires the life of a perfect man with no sin. Jesus Christ, God in the flesh, lives a perfect life on earth, so He alone can offer Himself as a ransom for our sins. Salvation comes at a cost that only Jesus was willing and able to pay.

Men choose to die for many reasons, but what would compel God to die for sinners? Love. For God so loved the world, that Christ sacrificed His life to save His enemies. Jesus Christ, innocent and blameless, dies the death of a criminal by Roman crucifixion, where He is beaten and nailed on a wooden cross to hang and suffer. The sins of all men are laid upon Jesus, who endures the penalty for sin so we can be forgiven by God. My friend, Christ died to save *you*.

It is finished, the price for our sin is paid, but Christ has died. A man can give his life, but no mere mortal can take it back from death. No man has ever escaped the grip of death with their own power. Only God has the power to overcome death. Since Christ is God, death has no power over Him. As Scripture states, on the third day after being crucified and killed, Jesus overcomes death and raises Himself back to life. Christ resurrects to show that He is no mere man, but God, and to give us the hope of life after death. Death was never the same after Christ died.

He. Is. Risen! Jesus is humanity's living and everlasting Hope, for what can a dead man do for you? Dead men bring nothing back to benefit the living. They may claim to be divine, but they are full of empty promises, as they are forever silenced by death's power. But Jesus is not like them, for while He lived among men, He claimed that He would suffer and die, but rise to life on the third day. If Christ has made good on such a promise, then He is to be trusted when He says that He is God; He is to be trusted when He says He paid the price for your sins; He is to be trusted when He says that those who believe in Him shall not perish, but have everlasting life; and He is to be trusted when He says that those who do not repent and believe in Him will perish in their sins. We can put our faith in Jesus, and He will not fail us.

What great joy we have because of the good news! What great joy we have because of the gospel! From the early first century until now, the testimony of Christ has gone throughout the whole world to people of every nation, tribe and tongue, commanding all men everywhere to repent, calling all men to forsake the darkness we love, to abandon our allegiance to sin, and believe in the One who can save us from hell and give eternal life. Jesus will save all those who come to Him.

Repent and believe the gospel of Jesus Christ. So when sin clutches at our frail bodies, and death steals our final breath, we will be in a place where sin and death will never be. We will be where Christ is, who now sits in the highest heaven, crowned in glory. We will live forever, and forever at peace with God.

Men look for God in their own places, but God has only made salvation, forgiveness, freedom and everlasting life available in one Place, in one Person. For there is only one name in heaven or earth by which men can be saved, and it is the name of Jesus Christ, the Living Son of God. He is King over all, and the Saviour of the world.

The church is one nation under God, and it is upon this doctrine where God's church is founded and built. For I esteem no record higher than the record of God. The Bible holds the words of eternal life. All men of this nation depend on it for life and godliness. We will put our trust in the God of the Bible. We will place our confidence in the Maker of heaven and earth. Until we are forever with Him. Amen.

Enoch Deboss
March 15, 2021

I form the light, and create darkness: I make peace, and create evil: I the LORD do all these *things*.

ISAIAH 45:7 (KJV)

God moves in a mysterious way,
His wonders to perform;
He plants His footsteps in the sea,
And rides upon the storm.

Deep in unfathomable mines
Of never-failing skill,
He treasures up His bright designs,
And works His sovereign will.

Ye fearful saints, fresh courage take;
The clouds ye so much dread
Are big with mercy, and shall break
In blessings on your head.

Judge not the Lord by feeble sense,
But trust Him for His grace;
Behind a frowning Providence,
He hides a smiling face.

His purposes will ripen fast,
Unfolding every hour;
The bud may have a bitter taste,
But sweet will be the flower.

Blind unbelief is sure to err,
And scan His work in vain;
God is His own interpreter,
And He will make it plain.

William Cowper

CHAPTER 1

God Created Evil – Blasphemy?

> I form the light, and create darkness: I make peace, and create evil: I the LORD do all these *things*.
> **Isaiah 45:7 (KJV)**

God created evil, but no one wants to give Him the credit. I am not trying to create shock value. I don't say this with some naïve bravado. I say this with fear and trembling, because this is not a light statement to make. To claim God created evil – and be wrong – is not just a light accusation; it is a malignment of God's character. God does not like to be misrepresented; He reprimanded Job's three friends for this, as they did not speak of God "*the thing that* is right" (Job 42:7). Eliphaz, Bildad and Zophar misrepresented the LORD in their discussions with Job, and God's wrath was kindled against them.

If you're going to speak about God, His character, and other high mysteries, you better be correct. We can't presume on the deep workings of God like Job's three friends. Scripture needs to be rightly divided (2 Timothy 2:15). If I handle this nuanced topic flippantly, and fail to support this position with sound doctrine, I will misrepresent God, and I may have to give an account to God for getting this wrong. I want to demonstrate my awareness of that. I am not casually tackling this topic on a whim.

That being said, I stand by my initial statement: God created evil, but no one wants to give Him the credit. This is probably the most controversial statement to ever be put forth in Christendom, because almost every Christian disagrees with it — at least in the way it's been historically understood. The historic and prevailing position is evil was not created by God; evil came from another source, and it cannot be attributed to God in any way. Despite the prevailing consensus and its underlying theology, is this position biblical? If not, what is the biblical position on God and His relationship to evil? What are the implications of this biblical position? This book will try to unpack these difficult questions with the Bible.

Again, God created evil, but no one wants to give Him the credit. The first part of this statement would naturally raise eyebrows, but the latter half of this statement seems to be a gratuitous embellishment on who God is. By saying God wants the credit for evil implies that God is being robbed of something by not attributing evil as His creation. When taken together, I know your natural reaction is to wince at the thought, dismiss this statement entirely, or prepare to throw your proverbial stones and cry "Blasphemy!"

Blasphemy is evil speaking; it is slander or irreverent speech that is intended to injure God's good name. Even though I am speaking on evil and its Maker, God, I have no intent to speak evil of God. By speaking on evil, I earnestly desire to uplift God's name and highlight His goodness, because there is no argument I will offer in this book that will change this faithful and steadfast reality: God has always been, currently is, and forever will be good. Yesterday, today and forever, the God who never changes is always good (Malachi 3:6; Hebrews 13:8). That much is clear. My intent is not to blaspheme the LORD, and in the case that I do, may God forgive me.

So before you pick up your rocks, and wind up for the stoning, please read through this book in its entirety. Get your Bible open and wrestle with the Scriptures. Be a Berean and

CHAPTER 1 - GOD CREATED EVIL – BLASPHEMY?

search the Scriptures on whatever I say; see if my theological arguments and logical deductions properly line up under the biblical hermeneutic, where Scripture interprets Scripture, and Scripture confirms Scripture (Acts 17:10-12; 2 Peter 1:19-21). I believe my position will stand under examination and scrutiny, but I am not above reproach. We should only care about what the Bible has to say, not what I want to make it say.

Now would be a good time to mention that the contents of this book revolve around a "foundation" issue, not a salvation issue. Christian, you can go your whole life not knowing who created evil, or where evil came from, and still enter into eternity. This knowledge is not required for you to be saved. Ascribing evil as God's creation does not deny the essential tenets of the Christian faith: God is the Maker of all things, man is a depraved sinner in need of God's grace, and that grace can only be obtained by repentance and faith in Jesus Christ, the Son of God, who died for our sins and resurrected from the dead to reconcile us to God, and give us eternal life. The core of the gospel message will not be perverted or undermined by this book.

The creation of evil is not essential to salvation, but it is still a foundation issue; foundation issues are issues that build on our understanding of God and the Bible in the context of our lives. If rightly studied and understood, these foundation issues will build your faith (Jude 1:20), will better equip you as the Lord's workman (1 Timothy 3:16-17), and will allow you to further explore all that pertains to life and godliness in greater breadth and depth (2 Peter 1:1-12; Romans 8:35-39). Right foundations will lead to right doctrine, and right doctrine will in turn edify and lead to right responses. Building on the foundation may not be essential to salvation, but it is essential to our growth as Christians. Psalm 11:3 says, "If the foundations be destroyed, what can the righteous do?"

We are trying to lay and build on the right foundations. Here is the core thesis for this book: According to the Bible, God created evil, and though He created evil, God is still good. Evil showcases the goodness and purposes of God, while working towards the Christian's ultimate good. Evil was created for God's glory, and it is why He deserves the credit, for God Himself wants the credit for evil's creation. Evil is in good hands — in God's good hands.

When I define "evil", I'm referring to the concept of evil, the parameters of evil, and the forms and expressions of evil that have been outlined in the Bible. The concept, parameters, and the forms in which evil is expressed and manifest in our world were designed by God Himself. The reason it exists, and its ability to exist is because of God.

Think of it like an inventor going to a patent office. An inventor first comes up with an idea, then gives life to the idea with a tangible design; the designer outlines the blueprint, and defines their invention's purpose, functions and capabilities. Once the idea is properly fleshed out, and functions according the designer's intended purpose, the inventor goes to the patent office. The patent office is where you go to protect the ownership rights of your invention. By securing a patent, it bears record of the invention's connection to the designer.

God's creation of evil operates in the same way. God lays out the concept for evil; He maps out what it is, defines its purpose, designs how it will function and take form, and bears record of His invention through Scripture. The Bible is the patent office; Scripture gives God's concept of evil the stamp of approval, legitimizing God's authorship and rightful claim over the idea. If God doesn't draw up schematics and functional parameters for evil, evil could never be what it is.

Without God, evil would never reach the patent office; it could not be an idea supported by Scripture, nor would it be

CHAPTER 1 - GOD CREATED EVIL — BLASPHEMY?

something that could be experienced by us in our present world, because evil wouldn't exist (Colossians 1:16-17). Therefore, any claims for God creating evil can only be legitimized with Scripture. I would not be able to support my position by any other measure.

Ultimately, the goal of this book is to bring you in awe of God, despite this controversial truth. Instead of striving against God, I pray this truth will edify and humble us, and cause us to glorify God, because evil was made for His glory. Proper theology leads to doxology. Sound doctrine will *always* compel us to praise the grace and goodness of God, which I hope this book will do.

This Book Is Not For You... Yet
As you may have expected from the first few pages, this is a heavy and complex topic. This book is not meant to be read by everyone, at least not yet. First, if you are not a Christian, you must put this book down. This book is meant for those who are born again, those who put their faith in Jesus Christ, and have been given new eyes and ears to discern spiritual truth. As an unbeliever, you do not have the spiritual capacity to receive these biblical truths in a beneficial way. This book may offer you gems and pearls, but you will not understand nor see the value of these things; you will trample upon these precious things like swine (Matthew 7:6). Before learning about evil, your first priority is to hear the gospel, believe in Jesus Christ, devote yourself to a Bible-teaching church, and learn the basics of the Christian faith. If you want to hear the gospel, I've written a thorough presentation of it as the foreword of this book. Start and go from there. Reading this book without being saved will do more harm than good.

Secondly, if you are a Christian, but you are relatively new to the Christian faith, I would also ask that you set this book aside for now. We will be taking deep dives into theology. A lot of advanced concepts will be explored, and discussions will not focus on the elementary principles of Scripture. To get the most out this book, you need to be skillful in dividing and handling the Scriptures. A basic understanding of the gospel will not be enough. If you can't understand the entire book of Romans, and cross-reference its content to other parts of the Bible, you are not ready to take on this book yet.

I reference your understanding of Romans because Romans is the essay of the Bible; it is Paul's Spirit-inspired treatise on the gospel from beginning to end. In it, we are presented with human depravity, condemnation by God's law, justification by faith alone, the heritage of righteousness and faith, the righteousness of Jesus unto salvation, reconciliation to God, our vicarious death to sin, our vicarious new life unto God, spiritual slavery, the persistence of the flesh, the power of the Holy Spirit, predestination, justification again, sanctification, glorification, the assurance of God's love, election, Israel's spiritual blindness, understanding the perfect will of God, and some practical ways we can glorify God.

Romans pulls back the curtain on the salvation you have received, and shows you how all these concepts work together for God's glory and your good. If you are unfamiliar with the topics above, or have a hard time grasping a majority of them, I wouldn't tackle this book just yet. You are still maturing in your faith.

This is not meant to offend you, but protect you. There is a time for everything (Ecclesiastes 3:1). Right now, as a spiritual babe in Christ, you may be thriving on the sincere milk of word — the basic truths of Scripture (1 Peter 2:2). It might be dangerous to introduce you to spiritual meat before you're ready (Hebrews 5:12-14). If you give a baby with no teeth meat to eat, they won't be able to break it down, and they may choke on the food. They were not mature enough to handle this kind of food yet. Spiritual meat is given to those who are mature enough to handle it; it is given to those with the spiritual teeth and tact (discernment) to properly receive it. Like the unbeliever, this book can result in more harm than good for the spiritually-young Christian.

George Whitfield said, "Let a man go to the grammar school of faith and repentance, before he goes to the university of election and predestination." Young Christian, I know you may be zealous, but before you sink your teeth into this strong meat, familiarize yourself with the basics. Hold fast to sound doctrine, and build upon it line upon line, precept upon precept (Isaiah 28:9-13). Eventually, you will move from milk to meat, and afterwards, you can come back to this book, and feast upon its contents with your spiritually-matured faculties. Your patience will reward you in dividends.

Isaiah 45:7 Made Me Do It
Years ago (as early as 2017), I stumbled across Isaiah 45:7. This verse is what motivated me to write this book. Isaiah 45:7 says, "I form the light, and create darkness: I make peace, and create evil: I the LORD do all these *things*." As you might expect, I was taken aback. I had never seen a statement like this in Scripture before. God saying He creates evil? How can this be? That statement appears to go against every thing I know to be true about God. God is good, so how could He create evil? How could evil come from a good God? That doesn't make any sense.

I wrestled with the verse for a while, and searched the Scriptures for other passages that would confirm my bias, and tried to build a case for both sides of the argument. In the end, I felt I didn't have enough evidence in support of God creating evil, so I tabled the topic for another time. Years passed until I would circle back to this verse, and reconsider the possibility. Up until then, I lightly broached the topic via the blogs, videos and sermons of different pastors and theologians, but no one seemed to present a biblically-robust argument for evil and its origins. The answers within Christian circles felt obscure and inconclusive, especially in light of Isaiah 45:7.

Here is God explicitly saying He creates evil, but many well-intentioned and respectable Christians have concluded that God did not create evil — without even acknowledging Isaiah 45:7. Or if they do acknowledge Isaiah 45:7, they refute it with theological gymnastics to distance God from the statement He explicitly made. Inevitably, things weren't adding up because we weren't taking God at His word. We were pulling out a piece of the theological puzzle, thinking we could see the whole picture on the biblical mystery of evil. But that only obscures the picture; it provides no clarity. All the pieces must be present for the picture to be clear.

God is saying He created it, man is saying He didn't. Who is right? Well, let God be true, and every man — including the well-intentioned Christian — a liar (Romans 3:4). God says He creates evil, and He is not shying away from it; He associates the act as His handiwork, and puts that on His name, for He the LORD does "all these *things*." The LORD speaks righteousness and declares things that are right (Isaiah 45:19), and God is not a man that He should lie (Numbers 23:19). Therefore, if He said it, I believe it; I must take Him at His word, regardless of the contrary arguments Christians put forth. Upholding the inconvenient truth of Isaiah 45:7 is vital to properly understanding evil in light of all Scripture. Now we have all the pieces to get the whole picture.

Obviously, I don't intend to build my entire argument off of this one verse. Scripture must interpret Scripture, and Scripture must confirm Scripture. Isaiah 45:7 is my fire-starter;

it sparked the premise behind this book. This verse is our starting point, and we will conduct a full breakdown of it in Chapter 4. And with the next two chapters, we will lay the groundwork to prepare ourselves for this.

If God is not sheepish about creating evil, why are we? Because it will force us to undergo a paradigm shift; it might change the things we believe about God, and challenge the presuppositions we have about ourselves and the world we live in. But if some of those beliefs are false, they are better off being replaced with truth and sound doctrine. As we expand and build a biblical case, God creating evil may not be as blasphemous as it sounds. May God be glorified.

O the depth of the riches both of the wisdom and knowledge of God! how unsearchable *are* his judgments, and his ways past finding out! For who hath known the mind of the Lord? or who hath been his counsellor? Or who hath first given to him, and it shall be recompensed unto him again? For of him, and through him, and to him, *are* all things: to whom *be* glory for ever. Amen.

ROMANS 11:33-36 (KJV)

Sovereign ruler of the skies,
Ever gracious, ever wise,
All our times are in Thy hand,
All events at Thy command.

He that formed us in the womb,
He shall guide us to the tomb;
All our ways shall ever be
Ordered by His wise decree.

Times of sickness, times of health,
Blighting want and cheerful wealth,
All our pleasures, all our pains,
Come, and end, as God ordains.

May we always own Thy hand,
Still to Thee surrendered stand,
Know that Thou art God alone,
We and ours are all Thy own!

John Ryland

CHAPTER 2

Three Good Doctrines You Need For Evil (Part 1)

O the depth of the riches both of the wisdom and knowledge of God! how unsearchable *are* his judgments, and his ways past finding out! For who hath known the mind of the LORD? or who hath been his counsellor? Or who hath first given to him, and it shall be recompensed unto him again? For of him, and through him, and to him, *are* all things: to whom *be* glory for ever. Amen.
Romans 11:33-36 (KJV)

God created evil, but no one wants to give Him the credit. According to the Bible, God created evil, and though He created evil, God is still good. Evil showcases the goodness and purposes of God, while working towards the Christian's ultimate good. Evil was created for God's glory, and it is why He deserves the credit, for God Himself wants the credit for evil's creation. Evil is in good hands — in God's good hands. That is the thesis for this book, inspired by Isaiah 45:7.

If this thesis is to be proven true, three biblical doctrines have to be established beforehand. These doctrines are the pillars that my thesis must rest on; if these principles are not properly established, misconceptions and biblical error will abound. These precepts will be the framework for my argument; they will create the lens through which the picture of evil is made clear. When things seem convoluted or confusing, you can make reference to these first principles to ground and center you theologically, for these precepts will permeate the pages of this book — whether explicitly or implicitly. They will be your North Star to guide you.

Our three doctrines are focused on the following topics: God's sovereignty, man's responsibility, and God's preeminent purpose for creation. These topics are very controversial to Christians, but they are not controversial to God because the Bible fully supports these doctrines. Many of the Christians who refute them are rejecting sound doctrine, and in most cases, many of them have not properly studied these subjects enough to conclude that they ought to be refuted. They can be frustrating concepts to tackle and accept for the Christian, let alone the unregenerate sinner.

I think man is frustrated by these doctrines for a few reasons. First off, these doctrines are naturally harder to understand; they are the spiritual meat that may take a while to break down. Secondly, these doctrines put God at the center, and puts man on the fringe to revolve in the orbit of God's purposes.

At the heart of it, they reject the idea that man was made for God, not the other way around. These doctrines are the hammer that smash this veiled idolatry to pieces. The proud Christian will put this book down, not because the doctrine is false, but because these doctrines reveal that they are not the center of God's universe, and shows how weak and powerless they are. But regardless of how these precepts attack a Christian's preconceived sensibilities, each doctrine will produce a consistent result: Man will be humbled and his ego brought low, while God is exalted and His character shines bright like a crown jewel. Even as Christians, it can be hard and scary to grasp the lengths that God will go to for His glory.

CHAPTER 2 - THREE GOOD DOCTRINES YOU NEED FOR EVIL (PART 1)

But we should not fear these truths, for all of these doctrines are derived from what Scripture says. It shouldn't produce fear or offence in us, but peace, understanding, and greater confidence in God and His promises. Psalm 119:165 says, "Great peace have they which love thy law: and nothing shall offend them." Our Lord Jesus Himself said "blessed is *he*, whosoever shall not be offended in me" (Matthew 11:6; Luke 7:23). Offence to truth robs us of access to blessing; we shouldn't cut off that fountain of blessing just because the Bible offends us in some area. We do ourselves a great disservice.

To press on with the truth despite being offended requires great humility. It is a humility that only God can give; no man naturally possesses it, but biblical humility comes by the grace of God alone. The LORD resists the proud, but gives grace to the humble (James 4:6; 1 Peter 5:5). Biblical humility is properly understanding who God is in contrast to who we are, and posturing ourselves accordingly (Romans 12:3). It recognizes we are feeble and impotent men before a great and all-powerful God. If we lack humility, we can ask God to make us humble (Psalm 119:32; James 1:5; 1 John 5:14-15).

To grow spiritually, we must humble ourselves in the face of God's sovereignty, man's responsibility, and God's preeminent purpose. When we bring ourselves under God's mighty hand to be transformed by the renewing of our mind, blessing awaits, for the LORD delights in the humble and will exalt them (James 4:10; 1 Peter 5:6; Matthew 23:12; Luke 14:11; Luke 18:14; Proverbs 29:23; Isaiah 66:2). If you are willing to receive these doctrines, understanding evil will be a blessing to you.

We will make our descent into valleys of pride-busting theology, where our pride, unbiblical misconceptions, and presumptions must be broken and set aside. They cannot continue on the journey with us. Only humility can accompany us as we make our ascent upon the mountains of biblical truth. Once we ascend to the highest heights of this rocky terrain, the spiritual perspective we gain will leave us in awe of God and His Word. The beauty of God's grace will be in full view. We will be standing upon good doctrine, a firm foundation that will do much good in our understanding of evil. Are you ready to make the climb?

GOD'S SOVEREIGNTY

God is in control of all things, at all times, and all the things that God controls at all times were ordained or determined by Him from the very beginning. Everything God has ordained will be accomplished in the end, and no one or nothing will thwart His established plan. God does not only know the beginning, the end, and everything in between, but God has declared and determined the beginning, end, and everything in between:

> Remember the former things of old: for I *am* God, and *there is* none else; *I am* God, and *there is* none like me, Declaring the end from the beginning, and from ancient times *the things* that are not *yet* done, saying, My counsel shall stand, and I will do all my pleasure: - **Isaiah 46:9-10 (KJV)**

It's no mistake that God reiterates that He alone is God before introducing the concept of His divine sovereignty. God wants you to know because He is God, He is in control, and has every right to be (Isaiah 44:6-8). What He says, goes. Whatever He desires to do will be done (Psalm 115:3). If He declared it to come to pass, no one or nothing will stop it (Numbers 23:19; Isaiah 48:3; Daniel 4:34-35; Acts 5:38-39). God's sovereignty is an inevitable reality, whether we want to accept it or not:

CHAPTER 2 - THREE GOOD DOCTRINES YOU NEED FOR EVIL (PART 1)

The counsel of the LORD standeth for ever, the thoughts of his heart to all generations. - **Psalm 33:11 (KJV)**

God is in control, and His plan for all things — whether in time or eternity — has already been determined, and will come to pass according to His word, power and will (Job 23:13-14; Psalm 135:5-6; Isaiah 42:8-9; Isaiah 55:10-11; Ephesians 1:9-11). This is the first doctrine we have to grasp. This is the beginning of our theological descent into the valley.

To What Extent Is God Sovereign?
To what extent is God sovereign? And to what extent is divine sovereignty at play in our lives? For starters, God is absolutely sovereign. The LORD is unrestricted in His supremacy over His creation. All things were made by Him (Genesis 1:1; Job 12:7-10; Isaiah 45:12; John 1:3; Colossians 1:16-17; Hebrews 11:3), all things were made for His pleasure (Revelation 4:11), and all of creation bends and bows to His will (Genesis 1:2-3; Genesis 6:17; Genesis 8:21-22; Exodus 7-12; Job 12:15; Job 37-41; Psalm 33:6-9 Psalm 104-105; Psalm 135:7-9; Isaiah 48:12-13; Daniel 3:26-27; Nahum 1:3-7; Matthew 8:23-27; Matthew 27:50-54; Mark 4:35-41; Luke 8:22-25; Revelation 21:1).

Therefore, in His absolute sovereignty, God retains absolute ownership, authority, rule and control over all creation. Under this pretense, the LORD can do whatever He wants.

In Which Ways Is God Sovereign?
If God is absolutely sovereign, in what ways is His absolute sovereignty exercised? I've already provided Scripture references in the last section, but first and foremost, God is sovereign over all creation. Every inch and aspect of His universe — visible and invisible — is controlled and ordered by Him. Every facet of nature, every creature, thing, power, capability, capacity, and concept that exists is rooted in Him and sustained by Him.

Nothing that exists — good or evil — would exist without being sustained by the word of His power (Hebrews 1:1-3).

When it comes to creation, God is the Alpha and the Omega, the beginning and the end, the first and the last (Revelation 1:8; Revelation 1:11; Revelation 21:6; Revelation 22:13). All of creation begins and ends with God, for "of him, and through him, and to him, *are* all things" (Romans 11:36).

God is sovereign over eternity, time, and all events in history. God is sovereign over eternity because God is eternal (Deuteronomy 33:27; Isaiah 40:28; Jeremiah 10:10; Romans 16:25-27; 1 Timothy 1:17; 1 Timothy 6:15-16). Eternal is the quality of being timeless, unending, everlasting, or not being constrained to the effects of time. There is no time which marks God's beginning or God's end; from everlasting to everlasting, God has always self-existed as God, and will continue to forever self exist as God without end (Psalm 41:13; Psalm 90:2; Psalm 93:2; Psalm 102:23-27; Psalm 106:48; Isaiah 43:10-13; Habakkuk 1:12; Revelation 4:8-10).

As the eternal God, He embodies the essential property of eternity and eternal things. Everything that retains an eternal quality is derived from God Himself (Genesis 9:8-17; Genesis 17:19; Psalm 100:5; Psalm 103:17; Psalm 119:142; Psalm 145:13; Isaiah 26:4; Isaiah 45:17; Isaiah 56:5; Isaiah 57:15; Isaiah 60:19-20; Daniel 4:3; Daniel 4:34; Daniel 7:14; Daniel 7:27; Daniel 12:2; Matthew 18:8; Matthew 19:29; Matthew 25:41, 46; John 3:15-16; 2 Thessalonians 2:16; Hebrews 9:11-15; Revelation 20:10-15).

God's sovereignty over time begins with His creation of it (Genesis 1:1-5, 14-19). Since we've established God is eternal, He transcends time; He is not constrained to the boundaries and passage of time (Joshua 10:12-14; 2 Kings 20:8-11; Psalm 90:4; Malachi 3:6; Hebrews 13:8; 2 Peter 3:8; Revelation 1:1-2, 10-11). The Creator is greater than His creation, and time is no exception (Isaiah 60:19-20; Isaiah 64:8; Jeremiah 18:1-6; Romans 9:21-22). The LORD is the Potter and time is the clay which He shapes to fit His purposes (Acts 1:6-7).

With that in mind, every event in history is governed by God's decrees. When we look at history from a human perspective, it primarily consists of those in the present being forced to look in the past. Yes, we can try and *make* history by impacting the present (Esther 4:6-17), or make calculated predictions for the near and distant future, but none of these are actual guarantees to create history in the exact way we may envision it. As finite beings, that's as far as we can go in terms of directing historical events. We cannot go backward or forward in time to change anything. We are bound to the present. For man to mess with history in any other way is science fiction (i.e. time travel), or downright inconceivable to the human mind (John 3:3-7).

But with God, it's different. Knowing God transcends time, His influence on the linear course of history (past, present, future) is omnipotent and all-encompassing. The LORD doesn't have to wonder about His impact on all history, because He determines every event (Isaiah 46:9-10; Isaiah 44:6-8). God exercises His sovereignty over past, present and future events. History is in His hands; He directs its course as the rivers of water, and weaves it into a glorious tapestry. No event in history — good or bad — can occur unless it has been ordained by the LORD:

> God that made the world and all things therein, seeing that he is Lord of heaven and earth, dwelleth not in temples made with hands... And hath made of one blood all nations of men for to dwell on all the face of the earth, and hath determined the times before appointed, and the bounds of their habitation; - **Acts 17:24, 26 (KJV)**

Before time began, the epochs of history were appointed by God, and every event in history has its place at God's appointed time (Ecclesiastes 3:1-8, 11, 14). It is with His absolute power that God determined what will happen in history, and when.

As the Apostle Paul states in Acts 17, through history, God is sovereign over the nations (Psalm 22:28). Every nation that ever was, every nation that ever will be, their posterity as a nation, and their boundaries on earth was established by God. He determined all the nations that would ever exist in history *before* they actually existed. God is sovereign over every nation and their affairs; their growth, prosperity and destruction are all in God's hands (Job 12:23; Jeremiah 18:1-10; Deuteronomy 8; Deuteronomy 9:1-6; Daniel 2:31-43; Daniel 11).

The God of the nations exercises His will through the nations. God Himself sorted and divided the nations of the earth (Genesis 10). The LORD also scattered the nations, spread them out, and caused them to abide in specific places throughout the earth. This was done to stop man's attempt for global government at Babel (Genesis 11:1-9).

God will also be the catalyst in gathering the nations; as part of His eternal purpose, God will gather men from every nation into His heavenly kingdom for His glory (Revelation 5:9-10). God has ordained for the nations to be gathered together under the antichrist's one-world government, which Christ will destroy when He returns to earth to establish His global government and kingdom for 1,000 years (Revelation 13:1-8; Revelation 19:11-21; Revelation 20:4-6; Isaiah 9:6-7; Daniel 2:44-45; Daniel 7:9-27). After Christ's millenial reign, Satan will gather all the nations to fight against the LORD and His saints, but God will defeat them (Revelation 20:7-11). God wants to crush all of His enemies before establishing a new heaven and new earth (Revelation 21; 1 Corinthians 15:22-26).

CHAPTER 2 - THREE GOOD DOCTRINES YOU NEED FOR EVIL (PART 1)

If we take a more granular look, we see God's hand in moving the nations. I'll use Israel as a prime example. When the LORD established His covenant with Abram, He ordained that his descendants (the Israelites) would be enslaved in Egypt, be delivered from Egypt's affliction, and afterward return to inherit the land of Canaan (Genesis 15:7-21).

God brought about Israel's enslavement through the famine of Joseph's time (Genesis 41:28-37, 53-57; Genesis 45:5-8; Genesis 47:27; Genesis 50:22-25; Exodus 1:1-14). God ordered Israel's deliverance through Moses (Exodus 3; Exodus 12:31-42; Joshua 24:5), and in their conquest of Canaan, the LORD used Israel as the instrument to oust the Canaanites for the sins they committed in the land (Exodus 15:1-14; Leviticus 18:1-3, 24-30; Deuteronomy 7:1-11, 16-26; Joshua 11:15-23; Joshua 24:11).

Due to Israel's compromise with the Canaanites, the LORD was true to His promise, and caused the surrounding nations to afflict and oppress the Israelites for their evil ways (Leviticus 26:14-39; Deuteronomy 28:15-68; Deuteronomy 30:15-20; Joshua 23:11-16; Joshua 24:19-20; Judges 1:21, 27-36; Judges 2:1-3, 10-23; Judges 3:1-8, 12-14; Judges 4:1-3; Judges 6:1-6; Judges 10:6-9; Judges 13:1).

When idolatry persisted during Solomon's reign, God split the nation of Israel into two kingdoms — Israel and Judah (1 Kings 11:1-13, 26-40; 1 Kings 12:21-24). After years of rebellion and idolatry, these divided kingdoms were later led into captivity under Assyria and Babylon (Jeremiah 50:17; Ezekiel 23). The LORD stirred the king of Assyria to bring the northern kingdom of Israel into captivity (2 Kings 15:29; 2 Kings 17:18-23; 1 Chronicles 5:26; Isaiah 10:5-11), and raised up Nebuchadnezzar, the king of Babylon, to bring the southern kingdom of Judah into captivity (2 Kings 23:25-28; 2 Kings 24:1-5, 10-16; 2 Kings 25:1-21; 2 Chronicles 36:15-21;

Jeremiah 52:1-30). On multiple occasions, God referred to Nebuchadnezzar as His servant, and told all the kings and nations not to resist him, for the Lord had given Nebuchadnezzar power and authority over them (Jeremiah 27; Jeremiah 25:8-11; Jeremiah 38:17-23; Jeremiah 43:10-13; Jeremiah 46:25-26; 2 Chronicles 36:11-21; Daniel 4:28-37; Daniel 5:18-22).

> The king's heart *is* in the hand of the Lord, *as* the rivers of water: he turneth it whithersoever he will. - **Proverbs 21:1 (KJV)**

After 70 years of captivity in Babylon, when the Medes and Persians had conquered Babylon, God stirred the heart of Cyrus, the king of Persia, to make a decree to free the Israelites from their captivity and return to Jerusalem in Judah (Ezra 1:1-4; 2 Chronicles 36:20-23; Jeremiah 46:27-28). As He did with Nebuchadnezzar, the Lord makes it known that Cyrus is the one He has raised up, anointed, and commissioned to do His will, even though Cyrus did not know the Lord (Isaiah 44:28; Isaiah 45:1-6).

> Blessed *be* the Lord God of our fathers, which hath put *such a thing* as this in the king's heart, to beautify the house of the Lord which *is* in Jerusalem: - **Ezra 7:27 (KJV)**

This is just God's hand being traced in the history of one nation. God was sovereign over every battle and conquest among the nations that led to these events. He controls the chessboard, with victory and defeat in His hands. No war can be won, no conquest can be made unless the Lord grants the providence to succeed (1 Samuel 17:47; 2 Chronicles 20:15; Job 12:16-22; Psalm 20:7; Psalm 44:1-8; Psalm 75:4-7; Proverbs

CHAPTER 2 - THREE GOOD DOCTRINES YOU NEED FOR EVIL (PART 1)

21:31; Isaiah 31:1-3). This isn't just the case with Israel, but He dispenses judgment, victory, and defeat among the nations throughout history (Jeremiah 43-51; Ezekiel 25-33, 35-36, 38-39).

God is sovereign over man's life. God gave man his first breath (Genesis 2:7), He gives all men life and breath, and no life can be sustained without His hand, for all life begins with Him and belongs to Him (Job 12:9-10; Job 34:14-15; Psalm 104:30; Ecclesiastes 12:7; Isaiah 42:5; Daniel 5:23; Zechariah 12:1; Acts 17:24-25, 28). The LORD determined how you were born, when you were born, to whom you were born, your frame and disposition and where you would live, work, find love, and go to church (Psalm 139:13-17; Ecclesiastes 11:5; Isaiah 44:24; Genesis 25:24-27; Acts 17:26; Genesis 4:1, 25; Exodus 4:11; Genesis 5; Matthew 1:2-16; Luke 3:23-38).

It's a good time to mention that God is sovereign over the womb; He opens and closes it according to His purpose, and He can turn the barren womb into an oasis of blessing (Genesis 16:12; Genesis 18:14; Genesis 20:17-18; Genesis 25:21; Genesis 29:31; Genesis 30:17-18, 22-23; Judges 13:2-3; 1 Samuel 1:5-6, 19-20; Psalm 113:9; Luke 1:5-17, 36). God presides over the fate of every child that was ever conceived and born, and every child that was lost in conception and birth (2 Samuel 12:13-23; Job 10:18-19; Psalm 22:9-10; Psalm 71:5-6; Psalm 127:3; Isaiah 66:9; Jeremiah 1:4-5).

And when Rachel saw that she bare Jacob no children, Rachel envied her sister; and said unto Jacob, Give me children, or else I die. And Jacob's anger was kindled against Rachel: and he said, *Am* I in God's stead, who hath withheld from thee the fruit of the womb? - **Genesis 30:1-2 (KJV)**

In contrast to life, the LORD is sovereign over death. He reigns over death itself, and as the giver of life, He has every right to take it through death (Genesis 2:17; Genesis 3:19; Genesis 5:5; Deuteronomy 32:39; 1 Samuel 2:6; 2 Kings 5:7; Psalm 89:47-48; Psalm 90:3-12; Psalm 104:29; Ecclesiastes 8:8; Ecclesiastes 3:20; Revelation 2:18-23). The LORD God has marked out our lifespan, and is able to lengthen and shorten our lives (Exodus 20:12; Deuteronomy 5:16; Job 14:1-6; Psalm 39:4-5; Psalm 89:45; Proverbs 10:27; 2 Kings 20:1-11; Isaiah 38; Ephesians 6:1-3). You will live no longer or die any sooner than what God has allowed.

> LORD, make me to know mine end, and the measure of my days, what it *is; that* I may know how frail I *am*. Behold, thou hast made my days *as* an handbreadth; and mine age *is* as nothing before thee: verily every man at his best state *is* altogether vanity. Selah. - **Psalm 39:4-5 (KJV)**

In addition, God has already established how and when we die, and the circumstances regarding our deaths. When King Saul consulted the witch of Endor, the LORD prophesied Saul's death through Samuel, and it came to pass (1 Samuel 28:3-20; 1 Samuel 31; 1 Chronicles 10). For conspiring against Naboth, God pronounced death over King Ahab, Jezebel, and all of Ahab's house, which would come to pass in due time (1 Kings 21:17-29; 1 Kings 22:34-38; 2 Kings 9:30-37; 2 Kings 10:1-11). Jesus revealed to Peter the kind of the death he would die for the gospel's sake (John 21:18-19), and Christ Himself as God foretold of His death at the appointed time, which has been supported throughout Scripture (Matthew 16:21-23; Matthew 17:22-23; Matthew 20:17-19; Mark 8:31-32; Mark 9:30-32; Mark 10:32-34; Luke 9:21-22; Luke 9:43-45; Luke 18:31-34; John 12:27-33; Luke 24:13-27, 36-48; Isaiah 53; Genesis 3:15;

CHAPTER 2 - THREE GOOD DOCTRINES YOU NEED FOR EVIL (PART 1)

Psalm 22).

Death is an enemy, yet like all created things, death is God's servant who serves His purposes (1 Corinthians 15:22-26; Exodus 11:4-7; Exodus 12:12-13, 23, 29-31; Romans 5:6-10; 1 Corinthians 15:53-57; Isaiah 25:8-9; Hebrews 2:9-10, 14-15; Philippians 1:20-21; Colossians 1:17-22; 2 Timothy 1:10; Hebrews 9:15-17; 1 Peter 3:17-18; Revelation 1:18; Revelation 20:14). Death is at God's beck and call. On the cross, death stood at attention until Christ willingly yielded and "gave up the ghost" (Matthew 27:50; Mark 15:37; Luke 23:46; John 19:30). When the LORD summons death, it has no choice but to appear, and when God calls death to loose its hold, death has no choice but to relent (John 11:1-44; John 12:17; Acts 2:22-24; Revelation 6:7-8; Revelation 9:6; Revelation 20:11-13).

This is why the LORD is able to raise the dead (2 Kings 4:18-37; Ezekiel 37:1-14; Matthew 9:23-26; Matthew 11:1-5; Luke 7:18-22; Acts 9:36-42; Acts 26:8; Hebrews 11:17), and it is why God has the power to raise Himself from death (John 2:13-22; John 10:14-18; Acts 2:32; Acts 3:15; Acts 4:10; Acts 10:40; Acts 13:29-30; Acts 17:30-31; Romans 4:22-25; Romans 8:11; 1 Corinthians 6:14; 1 Corinthians 15:12-20; Galatians 1:1; Ephesians 15:17-23; Hebrews 13:20; 1 Peter 1:21). Jesus Christ is called the firstborn of the dead for this very reason (Colossians 1:18). Death sits under the feet of the Lord of life (Matthew 28:1-15; Mark 16:1-8; Luke 24:1-12; John 20:1-10).

Between life and death, God is sovereign over our earthly destiny. I alluded to this with God's sovereignty over man's life, but this point is a little bit different. As sovereign, God doesn't just know all of man's ways and goings (Psalm 139:1-6), but He has ordained and directed every step of our lives. The Bible mentions this over and over again (see next page):

O LORD, I know that the way of man *is* not in himself: *it is* not in man that walketh to direct his steps. - **Jeremiah 10:23 (KJV)**

A man's heart deviseth his way: but the LORD directeth his steps. - **Proverbs 16:9 (KJV)**

Man's goings *are* of the LORD; how can a man then understand his own way? - **Proverbs 20:24 (KJV)**

The steps of a *good* man are ordered by the LORD: and he delighteth in his way. Though he fall, he shall not be utterly cast down: for the LORD upholdeth *him with* his hand. - **Psalm 37:23-24 (KJV)**

Trust in the LORD with all thine heart; and lean not unto thine own understanding. In all thy ways acknowledge him, and he shall direct thy paths. Be not wise in thine own eyes: fear the LORD, and depart from evil. It shall be health to thy navel, and marrow to thy bones. - **Proverbs 3:5-8 (KJV)**

We truly do not order the course of our lives, nor were we made to. The things we thought were inside of our control, the things we felt were outside of our control, the things we thought were meant to be, the things we didn't see coming, and the things we perceived as complete missteps for our lives has all been accounted for in the journey God has laid out for us. Each facet of the journey was a step ordained by God.

Joseph understood this well; when he looked back at all the steps he took along the way — from being sent to Shechem by his father (Genesis 37:12-14), being redirected to Dothan by a stranger (Genesis 37:15-17), and being betrayed by his brothers to be sold as a slave in Egypt (Genesis 37:25-28). Even with his prosperity under Potiphar, Joseph remembered how he was falsely accused by Potiphar's wife and thrown into prison by Potiphar (Genesis 39). Despite the unjust circumstance, he remembered how the LORD prospered his way in the prison, and his encounter with Pharaoh's chief butler, who forgot Joseph's plight to be released after interpreting his dream (Genesis 40).

Joseph remembered how he was miraculously called up by Pharaoh to interpret his foreboding dream, which God used to save Egypt and make Joseph the ruler over all the land of Egypt, second only to Pharaoh himself (Genesis 41). All of these good and bad steps were ordered by the LORD, and were intended for a bigger purpose in Joseph's life. Joseph makes this sovereign reality known to his family multiple times:

> And Joseph said unto his brethren, Come near to me, I pray you. And they came near. And he said, I *am* Joseph your brother, whom ye sold into Egypt. Now therefore be not grieved, nor angry with yourselves, that ye sold me hither: for God did send me before you to preserve life. For these two years *hath* the famine *been* in the land: and yet *there are* five years, in the which *there shall* neither *be* earing nor harvest. And God sent me before you to preserve you a posterity in the earth, and to save your lives by a great deliverance. So now *it was* not you *that* sent me hither, but God: and he hath made me a father to Pharaoh, and lord of all his house, and a ruler throughout all the land of Egypt. - **Genesis 45:4–8 (KJV)**

And when Joseph's brethren saw that their father was dead, they said, Joseph will peradventure hate us, and will certainly requite us all the evil which we did unto him. And they sent a messenger unto Joseph, saying, Thy father did command before he died, saying, So shall ye say unto

Joseph, Forgive, I pray thee now, the trespass of thy brethren, and their sin; for they did unto thee evil: and now, we pray thee, forgive the trespass of the servants of the God of thy father. And Joseph wept when they spake unto him. And his brethren also went and fell down before his face; and they said, Behold, we *be* thy servants. And Joseph said unto them, Fear not: for *am* I in the place of God? But as for you, ye thought evil against me; *but* God meant it unto good, to bring to pass, as *it is* this day, to save much people alive. Now therefore fear ye not: I will nourish you, and your little ones. And he comforted them, and spake kindly unto them. - **Genesis 50:15-21 (KJV)**

Joseph didn't understand God's sovereignty at the beginning, but he learned that the LORD was his Shepherd in the hills and valleys of his life (Psalm 23). Understanding God's sovereignty made Joseph tender, merciful, forgiving and more confident in God than ever before. We may not become the second-in-command in Egypt, but whatever our lot, God is sovereign over our earthly destiny and ordains the steps we take.

As a reminder, sovereignty does not just imply God's absolute rule and control, but also includes God exercising absolute power over the things He rules and controls. Since God rules and controls all things, He is able to exercise absolute power over all things within His sovereignty. The final aspects of God's sovereignty put this into focus even more, so keep this in mind.

To begin our final stretch of this doctrine, God is sovereign over the words in our mouth. Man cannot even utter a word without drawing on the breath God provides. Words and language were formulated by Him, and God demonstrated this at Babel when He took the one language used among the world's people, and confounded it (Genesis 11:1-9). The

CHAPTER 2 - THREE GOOD DOCTRINES YOU NEED FOR EVIL (PART 1)

language the whole world depended on to communicate became an incoherent form of communication; all the words, their meanings, the grammar, the syntax, and the contexts in which they were used disappeared completely, and God would form new systems of language at the tower of Babel.

If the people attempted to speak their previous native tongue, all that would come out in their speech — and all they could understand — would be the new language God had assigned to them. Words, speech and language are rooted in God's power, and men are powerless before it.

When calling Moses at the burning bush, the LORD informed us that He made man's mouth, and assured Moses that He would guide his speech when standing before Pharaoh, and would put the words they need for deliverance into Moses and Aaron's mouths (Exodus 4:10-16). When Balak employed Balaam to curse Israel, God first opened the mouth of a dumb donkey and gave the ass words to speak and communicate with Balaam (Numbers 22:21-33; 2 Peter 2:15-16).

Moreover, when Balaam attempted to pronounce curses over Israel, all that would come out of his mouth were blessings over God's chosen people (Numbers 23; Numbers 24:1-13). It's not that Balaam *would not* curse Israel — Balaam clearly showed that he was willing to do so — but Balaam *could not* curse Israel. Three times was Balaam constrained to bless Israel, for the LORD had put a word in his mouth that Balaam could not stray from even if he wanted to:

> And the angel of the LORD said unto Balaam, Go with the men: but only the word that I shall speak unto thee, that thou shalt speak. So Balaam went with the princes of Balak.
> - **Numbers 22:35 (KJV)**

The New Testament scriptures continue to support God's

display of power over man's words and speech. When Zacharias did not believe the angel Gabriel about John's birth, God took away Zacharias' ability to speak, and his speech only returned once John the Baptist was born (Luke 1:5-22, 57-64). After Christ raised Lazarus from the dead, the chief priests and Pharisees conspired to kill Jesus, and as they took counsel together, Caiaphas the high priest offered his insight among his fellow detractors:

> And one of them, *named* Caiaphas, being the high priest that same year, said unto them, Ye know nothing at all, Nor consider that it is expedient for us, that one man should die for the people, and that the whole nation perish not. - **John 11:49-50 (KJV)**

Caiaphas suggested that Jesus Christ dying would be beneficial (or expedient) for the Jewish people and the nation of Israel. Jesus Christ threatened the religious and cultural influence that men like Caiaphas, the scribes and Pharisees had over the Jews, so Christ dying would primarily benefit them. This group truly wasn't concerned with the Jewish people or Israel, for they first believed that Jesus would be the reason why they would ultimately lose their societal position and station (John 11:47-48).

So under the guise of achieving a greater good for Israel, Caiaphas assumed that Jesus' death would allow them to secure the power and influence they coveted, which they feared was slipping away. From their sinful human perspective, what Caiaphas suggested was music to their ears. Kill Jesus, save ourselves. But Caiaphas didn't realize what he was saying:

> And this spake he not of himself: but being high priest that year, he prophesied that Jesus should die for that nation;

CHAPTER 2 - THREE GOOD DOCTRINES YOU NEED FOR EVIL (PART 1)

> And not for that nation only, but that also he should gather together in one the children of God that were scattered abroad. - **John 11:51-52 (KJV)**

Wow! What Caiaphas said didn't come from his own mind, but it came from the LORD — God put those words in his mouth. What Caiaphas thought to be a wicked, master plan was actually the high priest's endorsement of Christ as the sufficient Atonement for sin, not only for the Jews, but for the whole world. Caiaphas was prophesying, and his prophecy was from the LORD, even though Caiaphas wasn't aware of it. God worked good through his speech, even though his intent was evil (John 18:14; John 12:32-33; Acts 4:1-12).

As a final point for this section, Christ assured his disciples that He — through the Holy Spirit — would give them the words to say when they are delivered before their adversaries, and are forced to give an answer for the gospel's sake (Mark 13:9-11; Luke 21:12-15). We see this become a reality with Apostle Peter in Acts 4, and with Stephen in Acts 6 and 7. Our God has all the say in what we say (Acts 2:1-13).

The LORD demonstrates His sovereignty over the acts of men. First of all, God is sovereign over all the *good* acts of men. In Hebrews 11, what many of us have called the "Hall of Faith", we see a collection of examples of those who had biblical faith in God, and how they demonstrated that faith in various ways.

While Hebrews 11 speaks to the essence and expressions of faith, the book of Ephesians speaks to the source of biblical faith. Faith is the gift of God (Ephesians 2:8). It was the case with the Old Testament saints as it is with New Testament saints in Christ. The gift of faith from God precedes any demonstration of faith. Without faith supplied by God, these great cloud of witnesses would have never been able to do what they did (Hebrews 11:1-2, 6, 39-40; Hebrews 12:1-2). Without faith, Abel would have never offered a more excellent sacrifice (Hebrews 11:4). Without faith, Enoch would have never walked with God and possess a testimony that He pleased God (Hebrews 11:5-6). Without faith, Noah would have never built the ark at God's command, and would have perished with all the world in the flood (Hebrews 11:7). Without faith, Abraham would have never left his home, sojourned to Canaan, and believed God when He said Abraham would inherit the land (Hebrews 11:8-10). If not for faith, Moses' parents would have never preserved his life in the midst of genocide, and Moses would have never resisted Pharaoh, would have never endured affliction with his kinsmen, and would have never went to deliver the Israelites from bondage (Hebrews 11:23-29).

You get the point. Through faith, God was sovereign over the good acts and exploits those in the Hall of Faith would perform. By faith, God was the catalyst for the virtuous things they believed and performed (Hebrews 11:32-40). These benevolent actions don't only apply to the Old Testament saints, but includes us as well, for in Christ, God has prepared good works (or good acts) beforehand that He has ordained for each and every Christian to walk in:

> For we are his workmanship, created in Christ Jesus unto good works, which God hath before ordained that we should walk in them. - **Ephesians 2:10 (KJV)**

The LORD has already determined all the good you will do as a new creature; it is already set in stone. What a comforting thought! God not only holds the power to spur us to good acts, but God is sovereign in protecting men from committing evil acts. For example, when Abraham and Sarah sojourned in Gerar, Abimelech the king of Gerar mistakenly took Sarah for himself, thinking she was Abraham's sister. Based on the context from Scripture, Abimelech intended to sleep with her as a wife or a concubine. Knowing that this act would harm all parties involved, the LORD appeared to Abimelech in a dream, and demanded that Abimelech restore Sarah back to Abraham (Genesis 20:1-7). Notice what God says in this dream exchange with Gerar's king:

> But God came to Abimelech in a dream by night, and said to him, Behold, thou *art but* a dead man, for the woman which thou hast taken; for she *is* a man's wife. But Abimelech had not come near her: and he said, Lord, wilt thou slay also a righteous nation? Said he not unto me, She *is* my sister? and she, even she herself said, He *is* my brother: in the integrity of my heart and innocency of my hands have I done this. And God said unto him in a dream, Yea, I know that thou didst this in the integrity of thy heart; for I also withheld thee from sinning against me: therefore suffered I thee not to touch her. - **Genesis 20:3-6 (KJV)**

God resisted Abimelech from having sex with Sarah, for she was Abraham's wife; the LORD prevented Abimelech from sinning. Whatever God did, however God interevened, whatever affections He dulled in Abimelech, or whatever obstacles He put in his way, God made sure that Abimelech would not have the opportunity to fornicate with Sarah. Matthew Henry said, "It is a great mercy to be hindered from committing sin; of this God must have the glory, whoever is the instrument." It is truly of the LORD's mercies that we are not consumed (Lamentations 3:22). Jude 1:24 tells us that God has the power to keep us from falling into sin, and when we invoke the Lord's prayer, we ask that our heavenly Father would "lead us not into temptation, but deliver us from evil", which implies God is able to lead us away from sinful temptations, and also deliver us from evil — not only the evil that surrounds us, but the evil within us that can cause us to sin (Matthew 6:13; Luke 11:4). Resisting and fleeing evil is a good act in and of itself. God is sovereign over all the *good* acts of men.

I've covered God being sovereign over the good acts of men, but that is only half of the story. God's sovereignty over the acts of men doesn't only involve the good acts, but includes the evil ones as well. Now we are getting into very deep, theological waters. God is sovereign over all the *evil* acts of men. Multiple examples in Scripture show this to be the case. By God's grace, I will try to be even more meticulous with the examples given.

I can start with Adam and the fall of man, but I will save this one for last. I've already spoken at length about Joseph and his brethren, so I'll be brief — the wickedness and betrayal of Joseph's brothers were ordained of God (Genesis 45:4-8; Genesis 50:15-21). God was sovereign over the evil acts of Joseph's brethren, and used it for good.

As Moses made his trek back into Egypt, the LORD gave him insight into what he would do with Pharaoh:

> And the LORD said unto Moses, When thou goest to return into Egypt, see that thou do all those wonders before Pharaoh, which I have put in thine hand: <u>but I will harden his heart, that he shall not let the people go</u>. - **Exodus 4:21 (KJV)**

God decreed that He Himself would actively harden Pharaoh's heart; the LORD actively hardened Pharaoh's heart so He could magnify Himself before Egypt, Israel and the whole world (Exodus 6:1-8; Exodus 7:1-6; Joshua 2:8-11). The Bible later reveals that this is why Pharaoh was raised up in the first place (Romans 9:17-18). God was sovereign over the sinful act of

Pharaoh hardening his heart to God. To glorify Himself, the LORD took Pharaoh's heart — which is the seat of man's desire and will — and hardened it so Pharaoh would become obstinate, and resist God's command in letting the Israelites go. If you think your eyes are deceiving you, and believe what God proclaimed was a fluke, Scripture continually affirms God's sovereignty over Pharaoh's evil actions:

> And he hardened Pharaoh's heart, that he hearkened not unto them; as the LORD had said. And the LORD said unto Moses, Pharaoh's heart *is* hardened, he refuseth to let the people go. - **Exodus 7:13-14 (KJV)**

> And the LORD hardened the heart of Pharaoh, and he hearkened not unto them; as the LORD had spoken unto Moses. - **Exodus 9:12 (KJV)**

> And the LORD said unto Moses, Go in unto Pharaoh: for I have hardened his heart, and the heart of his servants, that I might shew these my signs before him: - **Exodus 10:1 (KJV)**

> But the LORD hardened Pharaoh's heart, so that he would not let the children of Israel go. - **Exodus 10:20 (KJV)**

> But the LORD hardened Pharaoh's heart, and he would not let them go. - **Exodus 10:27 (KJV)**

> And Moses and Aaron did all these wonders before Pharaoh: and the LORD hardened Pharaoh's heart, so that he would not let the children of Israel go out of his land. - **Exodus 11:10 (KJV)**

> And I will harden Pharaoh's heart, that he shall follow after them; and I will be honoured upon Pharaoh, and upon all his host; that the Egyptians may know that I *am* the LORD. And they did so. - **Exodus 14:4 (KJV)**

> And the LORD hardened the heart of Pharaoh king of Egypt, and he pursued after the children of Israel: and the children of Israel went out with an high hand. - **Exodus 14:8 (KJV)**

We're not going to pretend we don't see what the Bible says. We see God working in Pharaoh again and again and again. God hardened Pharaoh's heart, which caused Pharaoh to sin against God. Even when the LORD is not mentioned, we know that every time Pharaoh hardens his heart, God is behind the scenes in each instance (Exodus 7:22; Exodus 8:15; Exodus 8:19; Exodus 8:32; Exodus 9:7; Exodus 9:34-35).

A good question you may be asking is, "If God hardened Pharaoh's heart which caused Pharaoh to sin, is God responsible for Pharaoh's sin?" The Bible tells us no, but I will elaborate more on this with the next doctrine we cover. As an appetizer, here is a principle for you to chew on: In all our good, God gets the glory for being the Source of it. In all of our evil, we take responsibility. I'm going repeat this principle multiple times, and expand on it in the next doctrine. Just keep this in your hearts for now. Let's explore the other examples.

When God wanted to bring judgment upon Israel during David's reign, the LORD stirred David to take an unnecessary census of Israel, unbeknownst to David:

> And again the anger of the LORD was kindled against Israel, and he moved David against them to say, Go, number Israel and Judah. - **2 Samuel 24:1 (KJV)**

Another account makes it known that Satan was involved in David's actions (1 Chronicles 21:1), but the fact still remains — God was sovereign over the sinful act of David conducting a census. God turned David's heart, and David sinned.

Prior to David's reign, God was sovereign over King Saul's death; because of his sin with the witch of Endor, the LORD through Samuel decreed that Saul would die (1 Samuel 28:3-20; 1 Chronicles 10). Observe exactly how Saul died:

> Then said Saul unto his armourbearer, Draw thy sword, and thrust me through therewith; lest these uncircumcised come and thrust me through, and abuse me. But his armourbearer would not; for he was sore afraid. <u>Therefore Saul took a sword, and fell upon it.</u> And when his armourbearer saw that Saul was dead, he fell likewise upon his sword, and died with him. <u>So Saul died</u>, and his three sons, and his armourbearer, and all his men, that same day together. - **1 Samuel 31:4-6 (KJV)**

Sadly, Saul died by committing the sinful act of suicide. The first book of Chronicles also gives us a look into Saul's death, but provides us with insight from God's perspective:

> <u>So Saul died for his transgression which he committed against the LORD</u>, *even* against the word of the LORD, which he kept not, and also for asking *counsel* of *one that had* a familiar spirit, to enquire *of it*; <u>And enquired not of the LORD: therefore he slew him</u>, and turned the kingdom unto David the son of Jesse. - **1 Chronicles 10:13-14 (KJV)**

Saul committed suicide, but this account tells us that God slew him. How can both of these things be true? Well, God was sovereign over Saul's evil act, even though Saul died by his own hand; Saul's final sin was the means through which God simultaneously slayed him.

God was sovereign over Judas' betrayal and death. During His earthly ministry, Christ made reference to Judas' betrayal as the fulfillment of Scripture:

> I speak not of you all: I know whom I have chosen: <u>but that the scripture may be fulfilled, He that eateth bread with me hath lifted up his heel against me.</u> Now I tell you before it come, that, when it is come to pass, ye may believe that I am *he*... When Jesus had thus said, he was troubled in spirit, and testified, and said, <u>Verily, verily, I say unto you, that one of you shall betray me.</u> - **John 13:18-19, 21 (KJV)**

> While I was with them in the world, I kept them in thy name: those that thou gavest me I have kept, <u>and none of them is lost, but the son of perdition; that the scripture might be fulfilled.</u> - **John 17:12 (KJV)**

At the time of these sayings, the only scriptures available was the Old Testament; therefore, Judas' evil actions were already written in Scripture, and decreed to be fulfilled in the Old Testament (OT). Prior to His ascension, the resurrected Jesus most likely made His eleven disciples aware of this when teaching them from the Old Testament:

> And he said unto them, These *are* the words which I spake unto you, while I was yet with you, <u>that all things must be fulfilled, which were written in the law of Moses, and *in* the prophets, and *in* the psalms, concerning me. Then opened he their understanding, that they might understand the scriptures,</u> And said unto them, <u>Thus it is written, and thus it behoved Christ to suffer,</u> and to rise from the dead the

the third day: - **Luke 24:44–46 (KJV)**

Judas' betrayal was among all the things that must be fulfilled from the Scriptures regarding Christ's sufferings; Judas was fated by God to be Satan's servant, and be the one to facilitate Christ's death by his betrayal. When he stood before his fellow disciples, Peter was later able to articulate Judas' role from the OT Scriptures:

<u>Men *and* brethren, this scripture must needs have been fulfilled, which the Holy Ghost by the mouth of David spake before concerning Judas,</u> which was guide to them that took Jesus. For he was numbered with us, and had obtained part of this ministry. Now this man purchased a field with the reward of iniquity; and falling headlong, he burst asunder in the midst, and all his bowels gushed out. And it was known unto all the dwellers at Jerusalem; insomuch as that field is called in their proper tongue, Aceldama, that is to say, The field of blood. <u>For it is written in the book of Psalms, Let his habitation be desolate, and let no man dwell therein: and his bishoprick let another take.</u> - **Acts 1:16–20 (KJV)**

Peter makes these references to Judas apparent from the OT, written hundreds of years before Judas was born (Psalm 41:5-9; Psalm 55:11-15; Psalm 69:22-28; Psalm 109:1-20; Zechariah 11:12-13; Genesis 37:25-28). God was sovereign over the evil actions of Judas in the fulfillment of Scripture.

Speaking of Peter, this restored apostle was once a foolhardy and zealous disciple, who scoffed at the idea of betraying Christ, but he didn't understand God's sovereignty at play (see next page):

Then saith Jesus unto them, <u>All ye shall be offended because of me this night: for it is written, I will smite the shepherd, and the sheep of the flock shall be scattered abroad.</u> But after I am risen again, I will go before you into Galilee. Peter answered and said unto him, Though all *men* shall be offended because of thee, *yet* will I never be offended. <u>Jesus said unto him, Verily I say unto thee, That this night, before the cock crow, thou shalt deny me thrice. Peter said unto him, Though I should die with thee, yet will I not deny thee.</u> Likewise also said all the disciples. - **Matthew 26:31–35 (KJV)**

And Jesus saith unto them, <u>All ye shall be offended because of me this night: for it is written, I will smite the shepherd, and the sheep shall be scattered.</u> But after that I am risen, I will go before you into Galilee. But Peter said unto him, Although all shall be offended, yet *will* not I. <u>And Jesus saith unto him, Verily I say unto thee, That this day, *even* in this night, before the cock crow twice, thou shalt deny me thrice. But he spake the more vehemently, If I should die with thee, I will not deny thee in any wise.</u> Likewise also said they all. - **Mark 14:27–31 (KJV)**

These are two gospel accounts of the same event, and Luke and John also provide their perspectives (Luke 22:31-34; John 13:36-38), but I want to focus on the passages above. They're dense and beautiful, so let's unpack it.

The Lord Jesus begins by telling his disciples that He will become a reproach to them, and this reproach will cause them to scatter like sheep without a shepherd. The disciples' forsaking of Christ was ordained of God, for "it is written" in Scripture, as Jesus had told them. This was a prophetic, Old Testament reference found in Zechariah 13:7. This forsaking

CHAPTER 2 - THREE GOOD DOCTRINES YOU NEED FOR EVIL (PART 1)

was inevitably fulfilled at Jesus' arrest (Matthew 26:56; Mark 14:50). It was written, so it would happen.

But Peter had other plans; Peter began to buck against Scripture, and told Jesus when the time comes or whatever the circumstance, he would never see Christ as a reproach, and would never forsake Him. Then, in a display of sovereignty, Jesus speaks to Peter about his three denials.

We have to remember something important here. We know when the LORD speaks about future events, He is not just passively telling us what He knows, but is actively determining what will happen from His declarations (Isaiah 46:9-10). So when Christ as God speaks, it is not simply as the One who knows the future, but as the One who determines it. God has sovereignly determined that Peter will deny Christ, and there is nothing Peter can do to change that.

But Peter, not truly understanding the power of God over his actions, proceeds to engage in one of the greatest displays of ignorance in human history. After hearing this supposedly outlandish claim, Peter becomes even more brazen, and tells Jesus that even if he has to die, he will still not deny Christ. Do you see the heart of what Peter is saying? Though well-intentioned, Peter is saying in not so many words, "Even though God has decreed my future actions, I will resist it. My will won't bend to God's sovereign decree. I will change the future from what God has said."

Now that Christ had told him of what he was going to do, Peter had the foreknowledge to guard against his evil actions, and simply change the future. Knowing what he was foretold, Peter could simply act against it, and not fulfill what Christ had said. How did things work out for Peter?

Well, what was ordained came to pass, for Peter denied Christ three times (Matthew 26:69-75; Mark 14:66-72; Luke 22:54-62; John 18:15-18, 25-27). In Luke's gospel, right after

Peter's third denial, as if it were providential and perfect timing — and it was — Jesus finds Peter and looks at him; God's sovereignty over man's evil actions come face to face, and Peter finally sees that he could not resist fulfilling God's inevitable decree. Peter learned that despite the "many devices in a man's heart; nevertheless the counsel of the LORD, that shall stand" (Proverbs 19:21).

Caiaphas, Judas and Peter's sinful actions are components which culminate into the most evil act of all — the conspiracy, wrongful indictment and crucifixion of Jesus Christ. Even in this, the Bible makes it explicitly clear that God was sovereign over the most evil act in human history. Apostle Peter and the early church understood this, and made it known to the world in the book of Acts:

> Ye men of Israel, hear these words; Jesus of Nazareth, a man approved of God among you by miracles and wonders and signs, which God did by him in the midst of you, as ye yourselves also know: <u>Him, being delivered by the determinate counsel and foreknowledge of God, ye have taken, and by wicked hands have crucified and slain:</u> - **Acts 2:22-23 (KJV)**

> And when Peter saw *it*, he answered unto the people, <u>Ye men of Israel</u>, why marvel ye at this? or why look ye so earnestly on us, as though by our own power or holiness we had made this man to walk? The God of Abraham, and of Isaac, and of Jacob, the God of our fathers, hath glorified his Son Jesus; <u>whom ye delivered up, and denied him in the presence of Pilate</u>, when he was determined to let *him* go. <u>But ye denied the Holy One and the Just</u>, and desired a murderer to be granted unto you; <u>And killed the Prince of life</u>, whom God hath raised from the dead; whereof we are

CHAPTER 2 - THREE GOOD DOCTRINES YOU NEED FOR EVIL (PART 1)

witnesses... And now, brethren, I wot that through ignorance ye did *it*, as *did* also your rulers. <u>But those things, which God before had shewed by the mouth of all his prophets, that Christ should suffer, he hath so fulfilled.</u> - **Acts 3:12-15, 17-18 (KJV)**

The kings of the earth stood up, and the rulers were gathered together against the Lord, and against his Christ. For of a truth against thy holy child Jesus, whom thou hast anointed, <u>both Herod, and Pontius Pilate, with the Gentiles, and the people of Israel, were gathered together, For to do whatsoever thy hand and thy counsel determined before to be done.</u> - **Acts 4:26-28 (KJV)**

Christ being delivered, crucified and slain at the hands of wicked men was sovereignly determined and orchestrated by the Lord (Acts 2:22-23). Their wickedness towards Christ was the fulfillment of OT Scripture (Acts 3:12-15, 17-18). The evil workings of their hands against Christ was already worked out by the hand of the Sovereign God (Acts 4:26-28; Isaiah 53).

I promised we would get to Adam, and here we are. I saved him for last because I want to draw on points we've already established, and use them to support the fact that God was sovereign over Adam's sin and the fall of man. I've already mentioned that no event in history — good or bad — can occur unless it has been ordained by the Lord, for He determines every event (Isaiah 46:9-10; Isaiah 44:6-8; Isaiah 48:3). This includes Adam's disobedience.

Now God's sovereignty over Adam's sin is not explicitly stated in the Genesis account, but many Scriptures in the New Testament make it clear, even though it may be articulated in different ways. A great place to start is Ephesians 1, as it is a large passage, and I will refer to sections of it in the future:

Blessed *be* the God and Father of our Lord Jesus Christ, who hath blessed us with all spiritual blessings in heavenly *places* in Christ: <u>According as he hath chosen us in him before the foundation of the world</u>, that we should be holy and without blame before him in love: <u>Having predestinated us unto the adoption of children by Jesus Christ to himself, according to the good pleasure of his will</u>, To the praise of the glory of his grace, wherein he hath made us accepted in the beloved. <u>In whom we have redemption through his blood, the forgiveness of sins, according to the riches of his grace</u>; Wherein he hath abounded toward us in all wisdom and prudence; <u>Having made known unto us the mystery of his will, according to his good pleasure which he hath purposed in himself: That in the dispensation of the fulness of times he might gather together in one all things in Christ</u>, both which are in heaven, and which are on earth; *even* in him: In whom also we have obtained an inheritance, <u>being predestinated according to the purpose of him who worketh all things after the counsel of his own will</u>: That we should be to the praise of his glory, who first trusted in Christ. - **Ephesians 1:3–12 (KJV)**

This passage is beautiful. You can return to it again and again to find something new, but let's draw our attention to the underlined portions. Through the Holy Spirit, the Apostle Paul begins to unravel God's master plan which He set up from before the foundation of the world, from before the earth ever was and before there was an Adam. This master plan was once concealed, but God has purposed to make it known to us in Christ.

It has always been God's sovereign plan for all Christians to be chosen out of the world to receive redemption, forgiveness and adoption in Christ to the glory of God (John 17). There is no adoption in Christ without a broken relationship in Adam (Romans 8:14-17; Galatians 4:1-7; Colossians 1:12-13). There is no redemption in Christ without a debt and a price to be paid in Adam (Acts 20:28; Ephesians 1:14; 1 Corinthians 6:19-20; 1 Corinthians 7:23; Hebrews 9:11-12; Titus 2:13-14). There is no forgiveness of sins in Christ without the commission of sin in Adam (Colossians 1:14; Hebrews 9:22). The sin of Adam and the fall of man was necessary for us to one day receive every spiritual blessing in Christ, which God has always intended to make available to us (1 Corinthians 15:21-22).

Since the LORD determines every event, He determined in His sovereignty the appointed time of Adam's fall, and the appointed time of Christ's redemption from that fall. If the LORD had not ordained it, Adam would have never fell, and sin and death would have never entered the world. When Adam sinned, Jesus Christ did not haphazardly turn into God's backup plan for sinners — this was the plan all along. Christ saving sinners was the plan established from before the foundation of the world (1 Peter 1:18-21; Romans 16:25-27; Ephesians 3:1-12; Colossians 1:23-29; 2 Timothy 1:8-11; Titus 1:1-3). God is sovereign over the evil acts of men.

We're almost done with this doctrine; I have two more points to address, but they are arguably the most controversial aspects of God's sovereignty, but Scripture affirms them, so we're going to stand on God's Word. Penultimately, God is sovereign over evil itself, and every form of evil. Satan, sin, death, the flesh, the world, demons, wicked men and hell — whether it involves their creation, their functionality, their sustenance and/or their destruction, the LORD is sovereign over evil in every regard. Every form of evil serves God's purposes in some way or another. God-willing, I try to illustrate this point later on in the book, and it's the reason I haven't included any

Scripture references as of yet, but I will cite my sources when I provide my arguments on God creating evil. I didn't want this point to come out of left field later, so I just wanted to mention it now.

Last but not least, God is sovereign over man's spiritual state and destiny. This is gonna be a doozy, because this is the aspect of God's sovereignty that many Christians reject, and if they were being honest, an aspect of God's sovereignty that they despise to their core. But I'm not going to shy away from it. Let God be true.

What do I mean by this? From before the foundation of the world, in God's sovereign master plan (Ephesians 1:1-14), God has already determined the eternal destiny of every human being; He has already chosen those who would become Christians by grace through faith, and those who would be reserved for eternal condemnation in hell. Embedded within this exercise of sovereignty is the doctrine of election.

Let's focus on God's sovereignty over man's spiritual state first, then move to God's sovereignty over man's spiritual destiny. We've already spoken about Adam's appointed fall, but in that, we know that all mankind inherited sin and became subject to death, for Adam was our federal head, meaning he was the spiritual representative for humanity; his spiritual state was our spiritual state, and his lot became our lot, which is why not just Adam, but all men through Adam are under sin:

> <u>Wherefore, as by one man sin entered into the world, and death by sin; and so death passed upon all men, for that all have sinned:</u> (For until the law sin was in the world: but sin is not imputed when there is no law. <u>Nevertheless death reigned from Adam to Moses, even over them that had not sinned after the similitude of Adam's transgression</u>, who is the figure of him that was to come. But not as the offence,

so also *is* the free gift. <u>For if through the offence of one many be dead</u>, much more the grace of God, and the gift by grace, *which is* by one man, Jesus Christ, hath abounded unto many. <u>And not as *it was* by one that sinned</u>, *so is* the gift: <u>for the judgment *was* by one to condemnation</u>, but the free gift *is* of many offences unto justification. <u>For if by one man's offence death reigned by one</u>; much more they which receive abundance of grace and of the gift of righteousness shall reign in life by one, Jesus Christ.) <u>Therefore as by the offence of one *judgment came* upon all men to condemnation;</u> even so by the righteousness of one *the free gift came* upon all men unto justification of life. - **Romans 5:12-18 (KJV)**

<u>For since by man *came* death</u>, by man *came* also the resurrection of the dead. <u>For as in Adam all die</u>, even so in Christ shall all be made alive. - **1 Corinthians 15:21-22 (KJV)**

When Adam sinned, the *freed* will God gave to man became enslaved to sin; once humanity lost the privileges of a freed will, and came under the power and bondage of sin, it caused us to become depraved and inclined to evil, for we're spiritually dead on the inside (Ephesians 2:1-6; Colossians 2:13).

We can do morally good things outwardly in man's eyes, but in God's eyes, we can do no good thing (Psalm 14:1-4; Psalm 53:1-4; Isaiah 64:6; Matthew 19:17; Mark 10:18; Luke 18:19; Romans 3:10); our nature is corrupted to the core and distances itself from God (Genesis 6:5; Genesis 8:21; Psalm 10:4-11; Isaiah 59:1-16; Matthew 12:32-34; John 3:16-21; Isaiah 64:7; Romans 3:11-18). Whether we practice outright wickedness or self-righteous moralism, all men are under sin (Romans 2:1-12; Romans 3:23; Galatians 3:22; Ecclesiastes

7:20), and we are inclined to exercise the whims of our sinful nature (Jeremiah 17:9; Matthew 15:18-20; Mark 7:20-23; Romans 7:14-25). The unsaved sinner's will is a slave to the power of sin (John 8:34; Romans 6:16-17; Romans 7:5).

Because we are spiritually dead, and alienate ourselves from God because of our sin, we cannot truly see God as He is, and would never turn to Christ for salvation by our own, corrupted will:

> The wicked, through the pride of his countenance, will not seek *after God*: God *is* not in all his thoughts. - **Psalm 10:4 (KJV)**

> For our transgressions are multiplied before thee, and our sins testify against us: for our transgressions *are* with us; and *as for* our iniquities, we know them; In transgressing and lying against the LORD, and departing away from our God, speaking oppression and revolt, conceiving and uttering from the heart words of falsehood. - **Isaiah 59:12-13 (KJV)**

> And this is the condemnation, that light is come into the world, and men loved darkness rather than light, because their deeds were evil. For every one that doeth evil hateth the light, neither cometh to the light, lest his deeds should be reproved. - **John 3:19-20 (KJV)**

> But though he had done so many miracles before them, yet they believed not on him: That the saying of Esaias the prophet might be fulfilled, which he spake, Lord, who hath believed our report? and to whom hath the arm of the Lord been revealed? Therefore they could not believe, because that Esaias said again, He hath blinded their eyes, and

hardened their heart; that they should not see with *their* eyes, nor understand with *their* heart, and be converted, and I should heal them. - **John 12:37-40 (KJV)**

As it is written, There is none righteous, no, not one: There is none that understandeth, there is none that seeketh after God. They are all gone out of the way, they are together become unprofitable; there is none that doeth good, no, not one. - **Romans 3:10-12 (KJV)**

But if our gospel be hid, it is hid to them that are lost: In whom the god of this world hath blinded the minds of them which believe not, lest the light of the glorious gospel of Christ, who is the image of God, should shine unto them. - **2 Corinthians 4:3-4 (KJV)**

The Scriptures are evident. The reason we don't seek God is because we *can't* seek God. Our sinful natures have blinded us, and have caused us to reject Jesus as the Light and the gospel as the way of salvation, for we have a spiritual allegiance to sin, evil and darkness. The spiritual state we are first born into causes us to reject God, Christ and the light of the glorious gospel (Psalm 51:5; Psalm 58:3; Isaiah 48:8).

This is why we must be born *again*; Jesus explains this concept to Nicodemus in their night encounter:

Jesus answered and said unto him, Verily, verily, I say unto thee, Except a man be born again, he cannot see the kingdom of God. Nicodemus saith unto him, How can a man be born when he is old? can he enter the second time into his mother's womb, and be born? Jesus answered, Verily, verily, I say unto thee, Except a man be born of water and *of* the Spirit, he cannot enter into the kingdom of

<u>God. That which is born of the flesh is flesh; and that which is born of the Spirit is spirit. Marvel not that I said unto thee, Ye must be born again. The wind bloweth where it listeth, and thou hearest the sound thereof, but canst not tell whence it cometh, and whither it goeth: so is every one that is born of the Spirit.</u> Nicodemus answered and said unto him, How can these things be? Jesus answered and said unto him, Art thou a master of Israel, and knowest not these things? - **John 3:3-10 (KJV)**

If you want to receive eternal life, and enter God's eternal kingdom, you must be born again. To be born again means you must be spiritually born — or spiritually made alive — by the water and the Spirit. The "water" is the gospel, which is the word of God that informs a sinner of his guilt, and directs his attention to Jesus Christ; the water of the gospel cleanses and sanctifies, and prepares the way for a sinner to be born again by faith (John 17:17; Ephesians 5:25-27; Acts 15:7-9; Romans 10:8-17; Psalm 119:9; 2 Timothy 3:14-17).

The "Spirit" refers to the Holy Spirit, who moves upon the face of the gospel waters, and possesses the regenerative power of God. Through the gospel, the Spirit regenerates a man, and gives him the gift of faith to believe on Christ (Ephesians 2:8-9; Titus 3:3-7). Regeneration is the idea of the spiritually dead becoming spiritually alive again (Ezekiel 37:1-14); it is having the light of the glorious gospel shine in our hearts and minds, so we can see Christ as He is, and profess Him as the Son of God and the only Way of salvation (2 Corinthians 4:3-4; Matthew 16:13-17; John 6:66-69; 1 John 2:22-25; John 14:5-6; John 1:13-14; John 6:40; John 5:21-24).

As Christ spoke on being born again, He called Nicodemus a master of Israel, which was a title for those who were educated in the Old Testament Scriptures, which implies that there are

CHAPTER 2 - THREE GOOD DOCTRINES YOU NEED FOR EVIL (PART 1)

OT Scriptures which allude to the new birth, and there are:

> Thus saith the Lord God unto these bones; <u>Behold, I will cause breath to enter into you, and ye shall live:</u> And I will lay sinews upon you, and will bring up flesh upon you, and cover you with skin, <u>and put breath in you, and ye shall live; and ye shall know that I *am* the Lord</u>... And ye shall know that I *am* the Lord, when I have opened your graves, O my people, and brought you up out of your graves, <u>And shall put my spirit in you, and ye shall live, and I shall place you in your own land: then shall ye know that I the Lord have spoken</u> *it*, <u>and performed</u> *it*, <u>saith the Lord.</u> - **Ezekiel 37:5-6, 13-14 (KJV)**

> For I will take you from among the heathen, and gather you out of all countries, and will bring you into your own land. <u>Then will I sprinkle clean water upon you, and ye shall be clean: from all your filthiness, and from all your idols, will I cleanse you. A new heart also will I give you, and a new spirit will I put within you: and I will take away the stony heart out of your flesh, and I will give you an heart of flesh. And I will put my spirit within you, and cause you to walk in my statutes, and ye shall keep my judgments, and do them.</u> And ye shall dwell in the land that I gave to your fathers; and ye shall be my people, and I will be your God. - **Ezekiel 36:24-28 (KJV)**

> <u>And I will give them one heart, and I will put a new spirit within you;</u> and I will take the stony heart out of their flesh, and will give them an heart of flesh: <u>That they may walk in my statutes, and keep mine ordinances, and do them:</u> and they shall be my people, and I will be their God. - **Ezekiel 11:19-20 (KJV)**

Thou sendest forth thy spirit, they are created: and thou renewest the face of the earth. - **Psalm 104:30 (KJV)**

Create in me a clean heart, O God; and renew a right spirit within me. - **Psalm 51:10 (KJV)**

But this *shall be* the covenant that I will make with the house of Israel; After those days, saith the LORD, I will put my law in their inward parts, and write it in their hearts; and will be their God, and they shall be my people. - **Jeremiah 31:33 (KJV)**

Regeneration radically transforms a man inwardly, to the point that he becomes a new creature altogether (2 Corinthians 5:17); the Holy Spirit transforms our affections *for* sin, our allegiance *to* sin, and our relationship *with* sin. As a new creature, a Christian is now dead to sin and made alive in Christ (Romans 6:1-11; Galatians 2:20). The power of sin is broken, and sin no longer has dominion over us. Sin still has *residence* in us (Romans 7; 1 John 1:8-10), but it no longer has *dominion* over us as spiritual slaves (Romans 6:12-23; John 8:31-36).

Therefore, the water presents us with the truth, but the Holy Spirit gives us the heart to receive the truth, and be transformed by it. This is what it means to be born of the water and the Spirit — to be truly born again.

Because of our darkened spiritual state, we could never bring about the new birth by our own power. We couldn't even come to Christ to be changed, and this is why God has to draw us through the gospel, so He can bring about the new birth by faith:

Jesus therefore answered and said unto them, Murmur not among yourselves. No man can come to me, except the

CHAPTER 2 - THREE GOOD DOCTRINES YOU NEED FOR EVIL (PART 1)

> Father which hath sent me draw him: and I will raise him up at the last day... And he said, Therefore said I unto you, that no man can come unto me, except it were given unto him of my Father. - **John 6:43-44, 65 (KJV)**

> For by grace are ye saved through faith; and that not of yourselves: *it is* the gift of God: Not of works, lest any man should boast. - **Ephesians 2:8-9 (KJV)**

> So then *it is* not of him that willeth, nor of him that runneth, but of God that sheweth mercy. - **Romans 9:16 (KJV)**

> But as many as received him, to them gave he power to become the sons of God, *even* to them that believe on his name: Which were born, not of blood, nor of the will of the flesh, nor of the will of man, but of God. - **John 1:12-13 (KJV)**

Your faith and salvation are a result of God's mercy, all wrought in God (1 Peter 1:3-5). You came to Christ because God *caused* you to come. You were transformed because God *caused* you to be. Your heart and will changed because God changed it by His power. The Puritan Jonathan Edwards famously said, "You contribute nothing to your salvation except the sin that made it necessary." Salvation is of the Lord (Jonah 2:9); God is sovereign over this process, and God radically transforms the heart and will of a sinner to make faith in Christ possible.

We can only come to Christ if God intervenes; man's spiritual state can only change if the Lord changes it (Psalm 119:32), and we have no control over it. With Nicodemus, Jesus describes the regenerative work of the Spirit as the wind; we have no over control the wind — we can't determine when it blows, where it comes from, and where it goes. We are simply subject to its effects as it blows. Repentance and faith in Christ is the effect produced from the Spirit's wind blowing on us at the appointed time (Acts 13:44-48).

For those of us who think the new birth involves us, I would ask you this: What aspects of your physical birth did you control? Did you control when you were conceived; how you were formed in your mother's womb; your looks, stature and temperament; when and where you were born; the parents to whom you were born to? You controlled nothing about your physical birth! God was sovereignly in control over these circumstances. The first birth is merely a shadow of the new birth (1 Corinthians 15:45-49). Be it the physical or spiritual, God works His sovereign power in both circumstances (1 Peter 1:22-23).

Some Christians hate the idea that God was sovereign over their spiritual state; they despise the notion that God changed their heart and will and caused them to believe on Christ. They don't like the fact that God overrides a man's will in their conversion. They think it's a violation of their free will.

As a rebuttal, I would kindly say this: So God shows mercy, but we shake our fist at Him because He intruded over our will to extend it to us? How prideful are we?! How dare we? What do we possess that does not belong to God? Life, breath and everything belongs to Him, including our wills. If God does not extend mercy, we would never repent and believe on Christ, we wouldn't even seek after God, and hell would be our deserving portion. God wants to turn our hearts to give us pardon and eternal life, and we are upset about the means He uses to do it?!

In our immaturity, we protest and cry out, "God invaded my will so I could escape hell, but I don't like that! It makes me uncomfortable! If God is gonna save me, He has to do it my way! He has to involve me in the process!" Respectfully, do you hear how foolish that sounds from someone who deserves nothing from God? This is the type of man-centric thinking that permeates our theology, and causes us to refute the sovereignty of God. This thinking is rooted in pride, and it needs to die. You are at God's mercy — humble yourself in light of that fact. Would you rather go to hell to protect your precious will? No Christian would take that deal. Instead of fretting over how God does things, we need to sit down somewhere and be amazed that God would ever offer us mercy at all. Selah.

> Man is nothing: he hath a free will to go to hell, but none to go to heaven, till God worketh in him to will and to do of His good pleasure. - **George Whitefield**

With that being said, I've digressed to the final aspect of God's sovereignty: God's sovereignty over man's spiritual destiny. God has already determined the eternal destiny of every human being; He has already chosen those who would become Christians by grace through faith, and those who would be reserved for eternal condemnation in hell. This expression of God's sovereignty is the doctrine of election.

Where do I even begin? Election is the doctrine of being chosen by God for a particular purpose. Election shows itself throughout the Bible, but it is explicitly mentioned in Romans 9, and explored further in Romans 11 and 8, so we'll start there. In Romans 9, the Apostle Paul uses Jacob and Esau as the case study for God's election:

> Not as though the word of God hath taken none effect. <u>For they *are* not all Israel, which are of Israel</u>... And not only *this*; <u>but when Rebecca also had conceived by one, *even* by</u>

<u>our father Isaac; (For *the children* being not yet born, neither having done any good or evil, that the purpose of God according to election might stand, not of works, but of him that calleth;)</u> It was said unto her, The elder shall serve the younger. <u>As it is written, Jacob have I loved, but Esau have I hated.</u> What shall we say then? *Is there* <u>unrighteousness with God? God forbid.</u> - **Romans 9:6, 10-14 (KJV)**

For some context, Apostle Paul is lamenting over the fact that a great majority of Jews in Israel rejected Christ, and he wishes that all of his kinsmen — the ethnic Jews — would turn to Christ, especially in light of all that they were exposed to in preparation for Christ (Romans 9:1-5; Matthew 3:1-12; Mark 1:1-8; Luke 3:1-18; Luke 24:45-49; Acts 1:1-8; Acts 2:1-41; Acts 13:13-49).

And while this grieves Paul, he understands that salvation is not wrought by what man desires or determines, but wrought in whom God determines to be called. Israel's genealogy and ethnic heritage does not entitle them to grace by faith, nor does it warrant their election, for God's sovereign mercy (and wrath) is the basis for election (Romans 9:14-18). Not all of *ethnic* Israel were chosen to be part of the *elected* Israel (Romans 9:6). The ethnic people of Israel were not the true Israel that the LORD ultimately aspired to form; the ethnic Israel was the shadow of the spiritual Israel that God is grafting into His adopted family in Christ, which is the Church (Romans 11:11-32; Ephesians 1:1-14; Ephesians 2:8-22; Ephesians 3:1-9, 14-15; 2 Peter 3:9; John 10:27-30; Acts 10:34-43; 1 Peter 2:4-10).

Understanding this, God showed Paul that election does not occur on the basis of who a nation is, but election begins at a personal level with God (Romans 11:1-8). This is why Jacob and Esau are used in the passage above; Apostle Paul reveals that God already determined how He felt about Isaac's twin sons, and already determined their earthly destinies. Before they were even born, and while they had not committed any good or evil as sinners, the LORD decided in His sovereign will that Esau would serve Jacob, even though it may have been contrary to normal customs (Romans 9:11-12; Genesis 25:21-26). Again, God's election does not conform to our wills, culture, customs, and expectations, but conforms to His will, His purposes, and His good pleasure (Romans 9:15-18).

Both twin brothers in equal states and stations were given two divergent destinies. God set His affections on Jacob, and chose for Jacob to be elevated above Esau, for God sovereignly chose to love Jacob, and sovereignly chose to hate Esau (Romans 9:13; Malachi 1:1-3). God's choice to love Jacob and hate Esau was not rooted in who each twin was, but was rooted in God's election — in who God decided to be chosen for their specific purposes.

This passage is laying forth the *principle* of election; in principle, election is God setting His love and mercy towards one person or group of people, and God setting His hatred and wrath towards another person or group. As Apostle Paul states, God choosing to sovereignly love one and sovereignly hate the other does not make God unrighteous, it makes Him sovereign (Romans 9:14).

Jacob and Esau are an example of God's election with implications according to the flesh, but the LORD wants to make it known that our salvation is an expression of God's sovereign election, which carries spiritual and eternal implications. This is laid out in the later passages:

What shall we say then? *Is there* unrighteousness with God? God forbid. For he saith to Moses, I will have mercy on whom I will have mercy, and I will have compassion on whom I will have compassion. So then *it is* not of him that willeth, nor of him that runneth, but of God that sheweth mercy. For the scripture saith unto Pharaoh, Even for this same purpose have I raised thee up, that I might shew my power in thee, and that my name might be declared throughout all the earth. Therefore hath he mercy on whom he will *have mercy*, and whom he will he hardeneth. - **Romans 9:14–18 (KJV)**

According to His will, purposes, and good pleasure, God arbitrarily elects to show one man mercy, and through this same election, God determines to show another man wrath by hardening their hearts — like He did with Pharaoh — and withholding mercy from them. Salvation is the dispensation of God's grace and mercy for those He elected for eternal life, and every Christian was drawn, called and regenerated through the gospel under this premise. On the other hand, those who rejected the gospel, and died in their sins to eternal condemnation had this grace and mercy withheld from them.

Because this appears to be unfair, it is highly offensive to the human mind that the LORD would actively choose to offer salvation to some, while withholding salvation from others. By withholding grace, God has essentially destined that man for hell. Knowing this truth would naturally invoke controversy among Christians, the Holy Spirit inspires the Apostle Paul to quell our misgivings about God's equity, and offers the rebuttal to end all rebuttals:

Thou wilt say then unto me, Why doth he yet find fault? For who hath resisted his will? Nay but, O man, who art thou that repliest against God? Shall the thing formed say to him that formed *it*, Why hast thou made me thus? - **Romans 9:19–20 (KJV)**

CHAPTER 2 - THREE GOOD DOCTRINES YOU NEED FOR EVIL (PART 1)

We can begin asking questions such as "If God is in control of my spiritual state and destiny, how can he hold me responsible for the very things He's in control over? Shouldn't His sovereign hand absolve me from responsibility for my spiritual state? And if He can show grace to every man, and transform their spiritual destinies by the working of His power and will, why doesn't He exercise His sovereign power over *every* man, so we can all receive grace, leaving no room for God to find fault with us since there's no condemnation in Christ? Why does He only save some, but not all?"

These are valid questions to ponder, and Paul begins by stating that the problem is not with the questions themselves, but with questioning God in the first place; our questions can subtly be the way we contend with God and how He does things. Paul first reminds us of our place.

As created beings, we are in no position to question the Creator (Isaiah 45:9-10). He has never needed a counsellor to guide His actions (Romans 11:34; Isaiah 40:13-14; Job 21:22). It is not for us to determine what should be fair; it is not for us to lecture God on how He dispenses His grace in salvation. It's for us to understand that God is God, and He does what He wants (Psalm 115:3; Psalm 135:6; Daniel 4:35). The LORD is transcendent; His ways are not our ways, and His thoughts are not our thoughts (Isaiah 55:8-9; Job 36:26). They are higher and better than what we can ever comprehend.

God is no man's debtor; He owes no man anything (Job 41:11; Romans 11:35). Since we are all under sin, if God was actually fair, all of us would be condemned (Psalm 130:3; Psalm 143:2; Romans 3:19-20). That is why salvation is called grace — it is the unmerited favour the LORD *never* had to bestow upon us, and it is the merciful kindness that the LORD was *never* obligated to show toward us. If God decided to condemn all of sinful humanity, and not make a way for us to become saved and made righteous, He would be perfectly right in doing so (Genesis 18:25; Psalm 145:17; Job 34:10-23; Exodus 33:19). But praise God He has made a way in Christ, and that to save some, if any at all.

In his commentary on Romans 9, Matthew Henry said, "All God's reasons of mercy are taken from within Himself. All the children of men being plunged alike into a state of sin and misery, equally under guilt and wrath, God, in a way of sovereignty, picks out some from this fallen apostatized race, to be vessels of grace and glory. He dispenses His gifts to whom He will, without giving us any reason... It imports a perfect absoluteness in God's will; He will do what He will, and giveth not account of any of His matters, nor is it fit He should... Whatsoever God does, or is resolved to do, is both by the one and the other proved to be just." Electing to save some, while electing to condemn others is within God's sovereign right to do, whether we like it or not.

Other than being disqualified as the creation, Apostle Paul continues to quiet our qualms with God, and drives the final nail in the coffin with these passages below:

> <u>Hath not the potter power over the clay,</u> of the same lump to make one vessel unto honour, and another unto dishonour? <u>*What* if God, willing to shew *his* wrath, and to make his power known, endured with much longsuffering the vessels of wrath fitted to destruction:</u> And that he might make known the riches of his glory on the vessels of mercy, which he had afore prepared unto glory, Even us, whom he hath called, not of the Jews only, but also of the Gentiles? - **Romans 9:21-24 (KJV)**

My goodness. No one but God could've said what was just said. Let's take a moment to break this down. Paul shifts the focus of the rebuttal from the creation to the Creator. Paul offers a set of rhetorical questions, and these are not simply Paul's speculative philosophies; these rhetoricals were inspired by the Holy Spirit, and authoritatively comes from the mind of God (1 Corinthians 2:9-16; 2 Timothy 3:16-17; 2 Peter 1:16-21).

As Creator, the LORD is the Potter which has the power to shape us — the clay — in whatever way He chooses, for whatever purpose He chooses (Isaiah 64:8). As the works of His hand, God has the sovereign right to prepare and appoint each man's eternal destiny, whether it be unto honour (eternal life) or unto dishonour (eternal condemnation).

> Is it not lawful for me to do what I will with mine own? Is thine eye evil, because I am good? - **Matthew 20:15 (KJV)**

Verses 22 and 23 reveal the preeminent purpose behind God's election: His glory. For those elected to be vessels of wrath, the LORD wanted to showcase the fulness and excellencies of His character, including His wrath and His power in judgment against sin and evil (Romans 2:3-6). God did this, even though it meant He would patiently endure the presence and terror of the wicked. They were fitted for destruction, and He would be the one to ultimately execute it upon them.

> The LORD hath made all *things* for himself: yea, even the wicked for the day of evil. - **Proverbs 16:4 (KJV)**

For those elected to be vessels of mercy, the LORD wanted to help these vessels understand the riches of His grace toward them (Ephesians 1:17-20). Understanding the fate of the vessels of wrath, while knowing we were once vessels of wrath ourselves, we all the more find beauty in the grace of being saved from that fate. God saved us unto eternal life, for which

He alone deserves all the praise and the glory (Ephesians 1:3-14; Isaiah 12:1-6; Psalm 118:14-29; 2 Thessalonians 2:13-14; 1 Peter 1:1-5; 1 Peter 2:9-10; Exodus 15:1-19; Psalm 18:2-3; Habakkuk 3:18; Psalm 62:6-8; Colossians 1:12-14; Psalm 77:7-15; Galatians 1:1-5; Psalm 86:8-13; Psalm 89:1-8; Psalm 98:1-9; Psalm 145:1-13; Revelation 7:9-12).

> Not unto us, O LORD, not unto us, but unto thy name give glory, for thy mercy, *and* for thy truth's sake. - **Psalm 115:1 (KJV)**

God elects and saves for glory — first to glorify Himself, and for us to glorify Him for the great mercy bestowed to us in salvation. Through election, there are vessels of wrath that were ordained to *become* vessels of mercy, and there are vessels of wrath who were ordained to *remain* vessels of wrath. For both purposes, God will derive His glory, and is to be praised.

> Some men cannot endure to hear the doctrine of election. I suppose they like to choose their own wives—but they are not willing that Christ should select His bride, the Church!
> **- Charles H. Spurgeon**

In light of this perspective on God's election, we shouldn't make a sport of presuming who are vessels of wrath, and who are vessels of mercy, for Paul warns against this (Romans 11:16-32); because of God's grace, who we presume to be vessels of wrath today may be revealed to become vessels of mercy tomorrow. From our finite perspective, no one's eternal destiny is written in stone. The LORD knows who He has elected, and it will be revealed to us fully after the Great White Throne Judgment, and after the second death is accomplished in Revelation 20 (John 5:22-29; John 6:37-40; Revelation 20:4-6,

11-15; Revelation 21:6-8). It is our job to faithfully plant and water with the gospel, so God the Holy Spirit can bring the increase of regeneration for those appointed to believe (1 Corinthians 3:5-8; 2 Peter 3:9; Acts 13:44-49).

For the Christian, election is merely the beginning of our eternal destinies taking shape; God's roadmap for our spiritual destiny continues beyond election, and finds its full formation in God's plan for us:

> And we know that all things work together for good to them that love God, to them who are the called according to *his* purpose. <u>For whom he did foreknow, he also did predestinate *to be* conformed to the image of his Son</u>, that he might be the firstborn among many brethren. <u>Moreover whom he did predestinate, them he also called: and whom he called, them he also justified: and whom he justified, them he also glorified.</u> - **Romans 8:28-30 (KJV)**

Our salvation is ultimately to God's glory, but there is an end goal for ourselves as well. In being elected, God's trajectory for us is to be conformed into the image of Christ, which means we continually internalize, embody, and express Christ's spiritual character within our being (Galatians 2:20; Romans 6:1-11; 2 Corinthians 5:14-15; 1 Thessalonians 5:9-11; Titus 2:11-14; Titus 3:8).

As we move from glory to glory (2 Corinthians 3:17-18; Psalm 119:32), are sanctified with the truth (John 17:17), have our minds renewed (Romans 12:1-3; Ephesians 5:25-27), are guided into all truth by the Holy Spirit (John 16:13-15; John 14:15-27; 1 John 2:27), and are partakers in the fellowship of His sufferings (Philippians 3:7-11; Romans 8:14-18), we are more and more conformed into the image of the Son of God; we come to know Christ more intimately, and we become more of what we behold (Exodus 34:29-35). We become as He is (1 John 3:1-3). This culminates into our glorification, where we are in God's presence forever — when we are finally free from sin's penalty, sin's power, and sin's presence altogether, and forever freed from all evil:

> And I heard a great voice out of heaven saying, Behold, the tabernacle of God *is* with men, and he will dwell with them, and they shall be his people, and God himself shall be with them, *and be* their God. <u>And God shall wipe away all tears from their eyes; and there shall be no more death, neither sorrow, nor crying, neither shall there be any more pain: for the former things are passed away</u>... And he said unto me, It is done. I am Alpha and Omega, the beginning and the end. I will give unto him that is athirst of the fountain of the water of life freely. He that overcometh shall inherit all things; and I will be his God, and he shall be my son... <u>And there shall in no wise enter into it any thing that defileth, neither *whatsoever* worketh abomination, or *maketh* a lie:</u> but they which are written in the Lamb's book of life. - **Revelation 21:3-4, 6-7, 27 (KJV)**

From election to glorification, the LORD is sovereign every step of the way. This is the entire purpose behind our salvation, and the aim of our spiritual destiny — the elect of God the Father being regenerated by the Holy Spirit in the hearing of the gospel of Christ, which is ultimately to the praise and glory of the Triune God (John 10:27-29; John 17:1-10; Romans 16:25-27). God is sovereign over our spiritual destiny.

> "To glorify God, and to enjoy Him forever," is the only worthy end of mortal man. - **Charles H. Spurgeon**

CHAPTER 2 - THREE GOOD DOCTRINES YOU NEED FOR EVIL (PART 1)

And there you have it; it took over 50 pages, but we managed to make it through a comprehensive exploration of God's sovereignty. It permeates the Bible to the same degree, with varying expressions and implications, but when we count the ways, God is absolutely sovereign according to the Bible. This is the first doctrine we need to understand evil. I will focus on the next two doctrines in the following chapter (Part 2).

The Poison Pill of God's Sovereignty

Before we close this chapter out, there is something we need to discuss. Our sin can cause us to die from a doctrine we were intended to live and flourish by. God's sovereignty is the preeminent doctrine in all of Scripture. It is the first good doctrine we need to understand evil. The sad thing is, we as evil human beings can pervert good things, including proper doctrine.

If we're not careful, our view of God's sovereignty can become unbalanced — or even unhinged — which can lead to pitfalls in our beliefs and behaviour. We can begin to postulate upon this doctrine and say, "If God is in control, then I don't need to do anything! Prayer is pointless. Whatever will be will be! If God is in control, then He is responsible for all the decisions I make, including my sins! If God is sovereign over man's spiritual state and destiny, then I don't need to evangelize to the lost, or teach my children in the ways of the LORD, for God has already determined their fates! What is the point of my choices when God is absolutely sovereign?"

Whoa, whoa, whoa. Not so fast! These are just a few examples, but do you see how fast an imbalanced view of this doctrine can spiral out of control? It can cause us to become presumptuous about God, which may lead us to commit presumptuous sins (Psalm 19:13). We commit the sin of Lamech with our wrong beliefs, thinking that one thing *must* mean another thing, or *must* lead to another thing (Genesis 4:19-24). Our wrong presumptions will skew our behaviour, and will make us lazy, apathetic, unfaithful and unfruitful Christians. Our calling is not to presume upon every aspect of our lives based on what we know about God's sovereignty; our calling is to glorify God, and obey His commandments (Matthew 22:26-40; Mark 12:28-34; Luke 10:25-28; John 14:15; Ecclesiastes 12:13-14).

Therefore, our understanding of God's sovereignty must be tempered with man's responsibility. In the midst of God's sovereignty, there is still a call to obedience and faithfulness on our part, which is what we will explore in the next chapter. Do not let God's absolute sovereignty become the poison pill you take to forsake your responsibility to be obedient, faithful, zealous and fruitful (Matthew 25:14-30; Luke 19:11-27; John 15:1-11). Amen.

I am not worthy of the least of all the mercies, and of all the truth, which thou hast shewed unto thy servant; for with my staff I passed over this Jordan; and now I am become two bands.

GENESIS 32:10 (KJV)

All that I was,— my sin, my guilt,
  My death was all my own;
All that I am, I owe to thee,
  My gracious God alone.

The evil of my former state
  Was mine and only mine;
The good in which I now rejoice
  Is thine and only thine.

The darkness of my former state,
  The bondage all was mine;
The light of life in which I walk,
  The liberty is thine.

Thy grace first made me feel my sin.
  It taught me to believe;
Then, in believing peace I found,
  And now I live, I live.

All that I am, even here on earth,
  All that I hope to be,
When Jesus comes and glory dawns,
  I owe it, Lord, to thee.

Horatius Bonar

CHAPTER 3

Three Good Doctrines You Need For Evil (Part 2)

I am not worthy of the least of all the mercies, and of all the truth, which thou hast shewed unto thy servant; for with my staff I passed over this Jordan; and now I am become two bands.
Genesis 32:10 (KJV)

With God's sovereignty out of the way (but in full view), it's time to tackle the last two doctrines for understanding evil: man's responsibility and God's preeminent purpose for creation. I assure you that my coverage of these doctrines will not be 50 pages long. I will try to be more concise.

As a reminder, the goal in exploring these three, biblical doctrines is to establish a firm foundation that will be used to prove my thesis, which I mentioned at beginning of Chapter 2. These doctrines are the pillars that my argument for evil will rest upon. Without them, this book has no ground to stand on. Let's continue with the second doctrine of the three.

MAN'S RESPONSIBILITY

While the LORD is absolutely sovereign, man is absolutely responsible for their actions and decisions. When Adam sinned, God held Adam responsible for his transgression against His commands (Genesis 2:15-17; Genesis 3:17-19; 1 John 3:4). God was sovereign over the event, but Adam sinned with his own freed will, which not only made Adam responsible, but made all of humanity responsible for the sin of one man (Romans 5:12-14; 1 Corinthians 15:21-22). Man was responsible for bringing sin and death into the world.

Even though Joseph told his brothers that the LORD was sovereign over their betrayal (Genesis 45:4-8), Joseph's brothers still took responsibility for the evil they did:

> And when Joseph's brethren saw that their father was dead, they said, Joseph will peradventure hate us, and will certainly requite us all the evil which we did unto him. And they sent a messenger unto Joseph, saying, Thy father did command before he died, saying, So shall ye say unto Joseph, Forgive, I pray thee now, the trespass of thy brethren, and their sin; for they did unto thee evil: and now, we pray thee, forgive the trespass of the servants of the God of thy father. And Joseph wept when they spake unto him. - **Genesis 50:15-17 (KJV)**

When God hardened Pharaoh's heart, which made Pharaoh obstinate in delivering the Israelites, Pharaoh rightfully recognized and took responsibility for his sin (even if it wasn't genuine repentance):

> And Pharaoh sent, and called for Moses and Aaron, and said unto them, I have sinned this time: the LORD *is* righteous, and I and my people *are* wicked. - **Exodus 9:27 (KJV)**

> Then Pharaoh called for Moses and Aaron in haste; and he said, I have sinned against the LORD your God, and against you. - **Exodus 10:16 (KJV)**

CHAPTER 3 - THREE GOOD DOCTRINES YOU NEED FOR EVIL (PART 2)

God was sovereign over Pharaoh's rebellion, but the sin of rebellion laid at Pharoah's feet. There is a transcendent mystery in here. God postured Pharaoh's heart to sin, which caused Pharaoh to sin, yet God was not responsible for Pharaoh's sin — Pharaoh only had himself to blame. We *cannot* say that God caused or made Pharaoh sin, for the Bible tells us that God does not tempt or entice any man with evil:

> <u>Let no man say when he is tempted, I am tempted of God:</u> for God cannot be tempted with evil, <u>neither tempteth he any man: But every man is tempted, when he is drawn away of his own lust, and enticed. Then when lust hath conceived, it bringeth forth sin:</u> and sin, when it is finished, bringeth forth death. - **James 1:13-15 (KJV)**

In Pharaoh's case, his resistance to God's command was evil, but God did not tempt Pharaoh with evil by hardening his heart; instead, Pharaoh yielded to the hardening, and with his own depraved will and nature resisted the LORD, specifically because he was drawn away of his own lust and enticed, which brought about Pharoah's sin. Pharaoh's inability to resist the hardening of his heart does not diminish the full culpability of his sin (Romans 9:19).

This is the answer to the question that was asked in the last chapter: If God hardened Pharaoh's heart which caused Pharaoh to sin, is God responsible for Pharaoh's sin? The book of James tells us no — Pharaoh was responsible for his sin, even though God was sovereign over Pharaoh's evil act.

Because we are finite beings, and naturally tend to view events in the context of cause and effect, these doctrines seem to conflict, but they are biblically compatible; it is nothing more than a transcendent mystery beyond our comprehension (Romans 11:33-34). In this particular context, God transcends what we interpret as a natural cause and effect relationship (namely, God's sovereign determinations as the cause, and man's sinful actions being the effect), for God thoughts are not our thoughts, meaning we don't think alike, and God's ways are not our ways, meaning we don't operate the same way God does. God is truly transcendent (1 Chronicles 29:11; Job 9:1-11; Job 37:23; Psalm 90:4; Isaiah 55:8-9; Romans 11:33). This means that God exists apart from the universe, and He is not subject to the rules and limitations He created for the universe, nor are His operations confined to our perceptions, but are confined to His nature and His revealed will in Scripture (Numbers 23:19; Psalm 138:2; Hebrews 6:17-19; Titus 1:2; Isaiah 55:11; Psalm 119:160; Romans 8:28-30; Philippians 1:6). What *we* fail to understand in the shrouded, transcendent mystery between God's sovereignty and man's responsibility, God understands perfectly and executes perfectly according to His infinite understanding.

> Great *is* our Lord, and of great power: <u>his understanding *is* infinite.</u> - **Psalm 147:5 (KJV)**

What we can't wrap our finite minds around is perfectly and plainly understood by the God with infinite understanding (Deuteronomy 29:29; Daniel 2:22; Psalm 139:12; Ecclesiastes 11:5). With this in mind, God has drawn a transcendent line in His Word, and I can't go beyond it (James 1:13-15; Proverbs 22:28; Revelation 22:18-19).

In every biblical example provided, the LORD is sovereign over the sinful acts of His creatures, but He is not responsible for the evil acts of His creatures. Each creature bears responsibility for their sin, while God retains absolute sovereignty. God can move a man's will to where He does not tempt a man with evil, yet the man still bears responsibility for

CHAPTER 3 - THREE GOOD DOCTRINES YOU NEED FOR EVIL (PART 2)

his sin, like Pharaoh did (Romans 9:19). With man, it doesn't seem possible, but with God, all things are possible (Matthew 19:26; Mark 10:27; Luke 18:27; Genesis 18:14; Jeremiah 32:17, 27).

As a quick tangent, though God does not tempt any man with evil, the Bible tells us that He *does* tempt man, but God's temptation is not aimed at enticing us to sin; instead, God's tempting is simply Him testing us through circumstance, with the aim to deepen our faith, refine our character, and make us more like Christ (James 1:2-4; 1 Peter 1:6-9; 1 Peter 4:12-19; Job 23:10; Romans 8:15-18).

The LORD uses the hardships and circumstances of life to expose our hearts, and reveal if we will be faithful to Him or not. We see this with Abraham sacrificing Isaac (Genesis 22:1-12; Hebrews 11:17), we see this in the Israelites' 40 years in the wilderness (Deuteronomy 8:1-5), we see it in Job's trial (Job 1:6-12; Job 2:1-10; Job 9:29-31; Job 31:1-6, 35-37; Job 33:8-13), and we see it in Peter's three denials (Matthew 26:69-75; Mark 14:66-72; Luke 22:54-62; John 18:15-18, 25-27).

If we fail in the trial, the sins associated with that failure belong to us, and it should refine us in godly sorrow and repentance (2 Corinthians 7:8-11); if we faithfully endure and overcome the trial, the glory belongs to God, and we are refined in our endurance and deepened faith (Philippians 3:7-14; 2 Timothy 2:8-13; 2 Peter 5:10; Isaiah 40:31). Both scenarios ultimately work together for our good (Romans 8:28; Romans 6:1-2; 1 John 2:1-6).

> The sins of God's elect turn to their good... poison is by art turned into a medicine — [their sins] make them cry more upon Christ, love Him more with all their soul, desire more earnestly to be joined unto Him, use all holy means of attaining thereunto... - **John Trapp**

In all our good, God gets the glory for being the Source of it (James 1:16-18; Psalm 84:11; Psalm 128; Deuteronomy 8:6-18; Psalm 103-104). In all of our evil, we take responsibility. God's temptation is a refiner's fire (Daniel 3:16-30; Proverbs 17:3; Isaiah 48:10-11; Job 7:17-18), but the temptation that leads us to sin is a consuming fire (Proverbs 6:27). They are not the same, as each form of tempting applies different methods, and seeks to reach to a different goal. Okay, tangent over. Back to exploring man's responsibility in Scripture.

Though God moved King David to conduct a census of Israel, look at David's prayer to God after the census was complete:

> And David's heart smote him after that he had numbered the people. And David said unto the LORD, <u>I have sinned greatly in that I have done:</u> and now, I beseech thee, O LORD, take away the iniquity of thy servant; <u>for I have done very foolishly.</u> - **2 Samuel 24:10 (KJV)**

The LORD sovereignly turned David's heart, and was behind David's desire to number the people, yet David took full responsibility for his sin. Again, this is a transcendent scenario similar to Pharaoh's — God moving a man's will to act without tempting the man with evil, which results in the man still bearing responsibility for his sin. Regardless of the influences at play, David sinned through his own will and actions, and God rightfully punishes him and Israel for it (2 Samuel 24:11-16; 1 Chronicles 21:9-16). Even as the LORD executes His judgment upon Israel, David reiterates who is at fault, and who should bear the brunt of God's wrath:

> And David spake unto the LORD when he saw the angel that smote the people, and said, <u>Lo, I have sinned, and I have</u>

CHAPTER 3 - THREE GOOD DOCTRINES YOU NEED FOR EVIL (PART 2)

<u>done wickedly:</u> but these sheep, what have they done? let thine hand, I pray thee, be against me, and against my father's house. - **2 Samuel 24:17 (KJV)**

And David said unto God, <u>*Is it* not I *that* commanded the people to be numbered? even I it is that have sinned and done evil indeed;</u> but as for these sheep, what have they done? let thine hand, I pray thee, O Lord my God, be on me, and on my father's house; but not on thy people, that they should be plagued. - **1 Chronicles 21:17 (KJV)**

When the Lord slew Saul through his act of suicide, the sin of suicide rested on Saul alone, for he willingly took his hand to do that which is unlawful (Exodus 20:13), and took hold of a right that belonged to God alone (Deuteronomy 32:39). God was sovereign in allowing Saul's death to take place in the way that it did, as it was according to His sovereign purpose, but Saul sinned in violating God's exclusive right to give and take life (1 Chronicles 10:4, 13-14). God was sovereign, and Saul was responsible for his sin.

If you can remember from the last chapter, I spoke about how God led Israel's two, divided kingdoms into captivity under Assyria and Babylon. The Lord stirred the king of Assyria to bring the northern kingdom of Israel into captivity, and raised up Nebuchadnezzar, the king of Babylon, to bring the southern kingdom of Judah into captivity. God sovereignly used Assyria and Babylon as instruments of judgment upon the nation of Israel.

Despite being used as instruments to plunder Israel, God still held Assyria and Babylon responsible for the very captivities He sovereignly initiated and presided over. For their wickedness in the captivity of Israel and Judah, the Lord assured that He would throw His instruments into the fire:

> Israel *is* a scattered sheep; the lions have driven *him* away: first the king of Assyria hath devoured him; and last this Nebuchadrezzar king of Babylon hath broken his bones. Therefore thus saith the Lord of hosts, the God of Israel; Behold, I will punish the king of Babylon and his land, as I have punished the king of Assyria. - **Jeremiah 50:17-18 (KJV)**

The instruments of God's wrath were now the subjects of wrath, and God would rightfully recompense Assyria and Babylon for their sins against Israel and the Lord (Isaiah 10:12-19; Ezekiel 31:2-17; 2 Kings 19:20-28, 35-37; Jeremiah 25:12-14; Jeremiah 51:1-14). Being instruments of God did not dispel the evil actions of these nations; it simultaneously served as the basis by which God punished them.

Judas Iscariot was God's chosen vessel who was used by Satan to betray Christ, and God was sovereign over the evil actions of Judas for the purpose of fulfilling Scripture, as we've discussed. Yet, Judas is no stranger to being accountable for his grave sin:

> Then Judas, which had betrayed him, when he saw that he was condemned, repented himself, and brought again the thirty pieces of silver to the chief priests and elders, Saying, I have sinned in that I have betrayed the innocent blood. And they said, What *is that* to us? see thou *to that*. And he cast down the pieces of silver in the temple, and departed, and went and hanged himself. - **Matthew 27:3-5 (KJV)**

This passage teaches us many things. First, the Holy Spirit affirms the doctrine of man's responsibility, and inspires the author of Matthew's gospel to write that Judas "had betrayed him", irrespective of God's sovereign decrees. Judas' betrayal left blood on his hands, and a scarlet stain on his conscience. Secondly, Judas' God-given conscience smote him, and led to him repenting within himself, which implied Judas violated his conscience, and he felt the weight of doing something wrong.

Third, Judas outright confesses that he has sinned against God by colluding against His innocent Master, the Lord Jesus Christ. Lastly, Judas grieved his sin by suicide. Grief unto death by suicide is a sinful expression of feeling accountable for Christ's wrongful indictment; it was the twisted display of Judas feeling responsible. This was the sorrow that led to death (2 Corinthians 7:8-11). Judas' conscience caused him to repent within himself, not repent to God. Judas could have found himself at the foot of the cross in true repentance, but instead, his sorrow led to him sinning again, which led to his physical death and spiritual destruction. All signs from Scripture point to Judas being responsible for his sin.

Like Judas, Peter also experienced sorrow after betraying Christ, despite his desire to do otherwise, for Peter's denials were ordained of God (Matthew 26:31-35; Mark 14:27-31). Though Peter fulfilled God's sovereign decree, we see Peter display shame and sorrow for his actions:

> And Peter remembered the word of Jesus, which said unto him, Before the cock crow, <u>thou shalt deny me thrice. And he went out, and wept bitterly.</u> - **Matthew 26:75 (KJV)**

> And the second time the cock crew. And Peter called to mind the word that Jesus said unto him, Before the cock crow twice, <u>thou shalt deny me thrice. And when he thought thereon, he wept.</u> - **Mark 14:72 (KJV)**

> And the Lord turned, and looked upon Peter. And Peter remembered the word of the Lord, how he had said unto

him, Before the cock crow, <u>thou shalt deny me thrice. And Peter went out, and wept bitterly.</u> - **Luke 22:61-62 (KJV)**

At the heart of it, Peter wasn't considering the sovereign workings of God in this moment, but was looking at himself and his wretched state for betraying the Lord he said he loved, and would die for. His lip service and lack of conviction grieved him at his heart, and caused him to depart in shame and weep with bitter tears. These were expressions of Peter feeling accountable for his actions, for Peter was responsible for his sins.

To further support this, after Jesus resurrected from the dead, He appears to Peter and other disciples on the shore of the sea of Tiberias (sea of Galilee), and invites them to eat with Him on the shore (John 21:1-14). After their meal, Christ begins to question Peter's love for Him to reveal what was in Peter's heart:

> So when they had dined, Jesus saith to Simon Peter, <u>Simon, *son* of Jonas, lovest thou me more than these?</u> He saith unto him, <u>Yea, Lord; thou knowest that I love thee.</u> He saith unto him, Feed my lambs. He saith to him again the second time, <u>Simon, *son* of Jonas, lovest thou me?</u> He saith unto him, <u>Yea, Lord; thou knowest that I love thee.</u> He saith unto him, Feed my sheep. He saith unto him the third time, <u>Simon, *son* of Jonas, lovest thou me?</u> Peter was grieved because he said unto him the third time, Lovest thou me? And he said unto him, <u>Lord, thou knowest all things; thou knowest that I love thee.</u> Jesus saith unto him, Feed my sheep. - **John 21:15-17 (KJV)**

This exchange is beautiful. Christ wanted Peter to affirm with his mouth his love and allegiance; in as many times as Peter denied Christ, there he would confess Christ before men those same, three times. It was a redemptive and restorative act for Peter. But what I want us to notice is how Jesus did not use God's sovereignty to excuse or pardon Peter's actions; Christ goes at the heart of what Peter did, and uses this exchange to hold him accountable, for Peter sinned, and Christ wanted him to recognize that so that he could be restored and strengthened (Luke 22:31-32; Proverbs 24:16).

Despite Christ's death being sovereignly determined and orchestrated by God (Isaiah 53), God did not absolve the wicked for their involvement, but held these men responsible for Christ's wrongful death as an innocent:

> From that time forth began Jesus to shew unto his disciples, how that he must go unto Jerusalem, <u>and suffer many things of the elders and chief priests and scribes, and be killed</u>, and be raised again the third day. - **Matthew 16:21 (KJV)**

> And while they abode in Galilee, Jesus said unto them, <u>The Son of man shall be betrayed into the hands of men: And they shall kill him</u>, and the third day he shall be raised again. And they were exceeding sorry. - **Matthew 17:22-23 (KJV)**

> And Jesus going up to Jerusalem took the twelve disciples apart in the way, and said unto them, Behold, we go up to Jerusalem; <u>and the Son of man shall be betrayed unto the chief priests and unto the scribes, and they shall condemn him to death, And shall deliver him to the Gentiles to mock, and to scourge, and to crucify *him*</u>: and the third day he shall rise again. - **Matthew 20:17-19 (KJV)**

Saying, Behold, we go up to Jerusalem; and the Son of man shall be delivered unto the chief priests, and unto the scribes; and they shall condemn him to death, and shall deliver him to the Gentiles: And they shall mock him, and shall scourge him, and shall spit upon him, and shall kill him: and the third day he shall rise again. - **Mark 10:33-34 (KJV)**

Let these sayings sink down into your ears: for the Son of man shall be delivered into the hands of men. - **Luke 9:44 (KJV)**

Then Jesus said unto the chief priests, and captains of the temple, and the elders, which were come to him, Be ye come out, as against a thief, with swords and staves? When I was daily with you in the temple, ye stretched forth no hands against me: but this is your hour, and the power of darkness. - **Luke 22:52-53 (KJV)**

Ye men of Israel, hear these words; Jesus of Nazareth, a man approved of God among you by miracles and wonders and signs, which God did by him in the midst of you, as ye yourselves also know: Him, being delivered by the determinate counsel and foreknowledge of God, ye have taken, and by wicked hands have crucified and slain: - **Acts 2:22-23 (KJV)**

The God of Abraham, and of Isaac, and of Jacob, the God of our fathers, hath glorified his Son Jesus; whom ye delivered up, and denied him in the presence of Pilate, when he was determined to let *him* go. But ye denied the Holy One and the Just, and desired a murderer to be granted unto you; And killed the Prince of life, whom God

CHAPTER 3 - THREE GOOD DOCTRINES YOU NEED FOR EVIL (PART 2)

hath raised from the dead; whereof we are witnesses. - **Acts 3:12–15 (KJV)**

The kings of the earth stood up, and the rulers were gathered together against the Lord, and against his Christ. For of a truth against thy holy child Jesus, whom thou hast anointed, both Herod, and Pontius Pilate, with the Gentiles, and the people of Israel, were gathered together, For to do whatsoever thy hand and thy counsel determined before to be done. - **Acts 4:26–28 (KJV)**

Then answered all the people, and said, His blood *be* on us, and on our children. - **Matthew 27:25 (KJV)**

When the chief priests therefore and officers saw him, they cried out, saying, Crucify *him*, crucify *him*. Pilate saith unto them, Take ye him, and crucify *him*: for I find no fault in him... Then saith Pilate unto him, Speakest thou not unto me? knowest thou not that I have power to crucify thee, and have power to release thee? Jesus answered, Thou couldest have no power *at all* against me, except it were given thee from above: therefore he that delivered me unto thee hath the greater sin. - **John 19:6, 10–11 (KJV)**

Judas, Israel's elders, chief priests, and scribes, the people of Israel, Herod, Pontius Pilate, and the Roman soldiers (Gentiles) who executed His crucifixion all had a hand in putting Jesus to death. Whether Jew or Gentile, these men were held responsible for killing Jesus Christ. Pilate could wash his hands until his skin peeled off, but it would not erase his contribution in condemning the Lamb of God (Matthew 27:24).

Man's responsibility is not simply relegated to the past accounts of Scripture, but applies to our present calling in

Scripture, and our future hope in Scripture. There are six ways in which this doctrine is binding upon all men, or specifically applicable to Christians: the call to draw near to God, the call to receive the gospel, the call to preach the gospel, the call to pray to God, the call to live holy and bear fruit, and the call to obey Scripture. Let's look at each of these ways in more detail.

As a starter, man is responsible for drawing near to God in light of His existence. The LORD has testified of His existence through creation (Psalm 19:1-4; Romans 1:18-23; Acts 14:14-17), and has embedded His law in the heart of every man, which is manifest in our conscience (Romans 2:13-15). God has provided man with a sufficient witness of His existence, and we are to use this knowledge to seek Him out, draw near to God, and learn what He demands from us as His creatures:

> God that made the world and all things therein, seeing that he is Lord of heaven and earth, dwelleth not in temples made with hands... <u>That they should seek the Lord, if haply they might feel after him, and find him, though he be not far from every one of us:</u> - **Acts 17:24, 27 (KJV)**

> <u>But *it is* good for me to draw near to God:</u> I have put my trust in the Lord GOD, that I may declare all thy works. - **Psalm 73:28 (KJV)**

All men know there is a God (Romans 1:18-20). Unfortunately, because of our depraved sinful nature, we deny creation's witness and suppress God's existence in our hearts and minds (Romans 1:21-23, 25, 28), so instead of drawing near, we run from God, for we prefer to walk in darkness rather than light (John 3:19-20), and cannot draw near to God without His intervention (John 6:44). But the calling to draw near to God still stands for every man; our inability to draw near through natural revelation does not diminish our responsibility to do so (Psalm 95:6). No man could stand before the LORD and say they never knew Him, for every man possesses this natural revelation within themselves, which provides sufficient grounds for God to condemn a man (Romans 1:18-19; Romans 3:5-9). Even with our responsibility to draw near, God's witness throughout creation supplies enough to condemn a man, but not enough to save him. This leads into my next point.

All men are responsible with their response to the gospel. As Apostle Paul states, the gospel of Christ is "the power of God unto salvation" and where the righteousness of God is revealed (Romans 1:16-17). It is the only means through which men can obtain salvation and righteousness from God (John 14:6; Acts 4:10-12). Therefore, there is a call for all men to receive the gospel when it is preached to us:

> Now after that John was put in prison, <u>Jesus came into Galilee, preaching the gospel of the kingdom of God,</u> And saying, The time is fulfilled, and the kingdom of God is at hand: <u>repent ye, and believe the gospel.</u> - **Mark 1:14-15 (KJV)**

Now is the day of salvation (2 Corinthians 6:2). Each time a man is exposed to the gospel, it is his opportunity to respond, and it is his responsibility to respond properly. Like the rich man in hell, a sinner may never get another chance to repent and believe the gospel, and it would be their greatest regret (Luke 16:19-31). Every mockery, derision, contention and rejection of Christ condemns a man even further before God (John 3:17-19; 1 Corinthians 1:18).

Though a depraved sinner cannot properly respond to the gospel call, he is rightfully condemned for his rejection of the gospel call. Again, a sinner's inability to respond properly to the gospel does not negate their culpability in rejecting it. Sinners actively reject the gospel and Christ, and justly receive eternal damnation because of it. Sovereign election and regeneration aside, every sinner has a responsibility to believe the gospel to receive eternal life (John 6:28-29; John 17:3; John 3:14-16; Revelation 22:17).

> Also, remember whatever the doctrine of election may be or may not be, the Gospel gives a free invitation to needy sinners. - **Charles H. Spurgeon**

On the other side of the gospel call, Christians are responsible for preaching the gospel to lost and unregenerate sinners:

> And he said unto them, <u>Go ye into all the world, and preach the gospel to every creature.</u> - **Mark 16:15 (KJV)**

> Then opened he their understanding, that they might understand the scriptures, And said unto them, Thus it is written, and thus it behoved Christ to suffer, and to rise from the dead the third day: <u>And that repentance and remission of sins should be preached in his name among all nations,</u> beginning at Jerusalem. - **Luke 24:45-47 (KJV)**

As disciples of Christ, we are called to go out into the world, and call sinners to repentance and faith in Christ through the gospel. Now, we have no power to convert a sinner, but our gospel preaching is the means by which the elect are drawn to Jesus, and regenerated by the Holy Spirit (Romans 10:8-17; John 3:3-8; Acts 10:34-48; Acts 13:44-49; 2 Corinthians 5:17; John 4:39-42; Matthew 13:1-23; Mark 4:1-20; Luke 8:4-15).

In this age, the gospel is the means through which God gathers His elect for eternal life (John 10:25-29; 2 Peter 3:8-9).

CHAPTER 3 - THREE GOOD DOCTRINES YOU NEED FOR EVIL (PART 2)

Therefore, we are called to deploy this means of grace for this purpose. It is the way we enter into God's labour, and engage in the kingdom of God, for there is work to be done:

> Jesus saith unto them, My meat is to do the will of him that sent me, and to finish his work. Say not ye, There are yet four months, and *then* cometh harvest? <u>behold, I say unto you, Lift up your eyes, and look on the fields; for they are white already to harvest. And he that reapeth receiveth wages, and gathereth fruit unto life eternal:</u> that both he that soweth and he that reapeth may rejoice together. - **John 4:34–36 (KJV)**

> <u>Then saith he unto his disciples, The harvest truly *is* plenteous, but the labourers *are* few;</u> Pray ye therefore the Lord of the harvest, that he will send forth labourers into his harvest. - **Matthew 9:37-38 (KJV)**

> It is the whole business of the whole church to preach the whole gospel to the whole world. - **Charles H. Spurgeon**

There is work to be done in the mission field of our evil world, and when we preach, we join in the effort of advancing God's kingdom, which is to call whosoever will come to Christ for salvation and eternal life (John 3:16). And even if our preaching efforts appear to be unfruitful, we walk by faith in God, not in what we see (2 Corinthians 5:7). Regardless of the spiritual harvest we may or may not see, we are still responsible to obey the mandate, and faithfully plant and water with the hope that God will bring the increase:

> <u>I have planted, Apollos watered; but God gave the increase. So then neither is he that planteth any thing, neither he</u>

that watereth; but God that giveth the increase. Now he that planteth and he that watereth are one: <u>and every man shall receive his own reward according to his own labour. For we are labourers together with God:</u> ye are God's husbandry, *ye are* God's building. - **1 Corinthians 3:6-9 (KJV)**

We are not responsible to God for the souls that are saved, but we are responsible for the gospel that is preached. - **Charles H. Spurgeon**

God is sovereign over all time, but we are responsible in our time. Preaching the gospel is as much for us as it is for the lost. Preaching is a demonstration of faithfulness, and if it does no good in the hearts of sinners, it still works good in us!

His lord said unto him, <u>Well done, *thou* good and faithful servant: thou hast been faithful over a few things, I will make thee ruler over many things:</u> enter thou into the joy of thy lord. - **Matthew 25:21 (KJV)**

<u>Preach the word; be instant in season, out of season; reprove, rebuke, exhort with all longsuffering and doctrine.</u> - **2 Timothy 4:2 (KJV)**

But whoso hath this world's good, and seeth his brother have need, and shutteth up his bowels *of compassion* from him, <u>how dwelleth the love of God in him?</u> - **1 John 3:17 (KJV)**

The fruit of the righteous *is* a tree of life; <u>and he that winneth souls *is* wise.</u> - **Proverbs 11:30 (KJV)**

CHAPTER 3 - THREE GOOD DOCTRINES YOU NEED FOR EVIL (PART 2)

To further complement the previous principle, man is still responsible in his call to pray. In the face of the sovereign God, who has determined all events from beginning to end, we might begin to muse on the purpose and usefulness of prayer. If God knows all things, and has already determined what will happen according to His will, why would I need to pray if God is already going to do what He's going to do? I could not utter a word, and everything would happen as it should according to God's plan. Therefore, why bother asking, seeking, and knocking in prayer to God?

The answer is simple — because the LORD bids us to pray, which then makes us responsible to do it:

> But thou, when thou prayest, enter into thy closet, and when thou hast shut thy door, pray to thy Father which is in secret; and thy Father which seeth in secret shall reward thee openly. But when ye pray, use not vain repetitions, as the heathen *do*: for they think that they shall be heard for their much speaking. Be not ye therefore like unto them: for your Father knoweth what things ye have need of, before ye ask him. - **Matthew 6:6-8 (KJV)**

This passage is perfect evidence to showcase this. The sovereign God will continue to work out His purposes with or without our prayers, but God invites and commands us to pray, for God is willing to respond to our prayers and requests. Jesus says "when thou prayest", which implies there is an expectation from God for us to pray, and to make prayer a consistent practice. Jesus goes on to say that the Father who sees our prayers in secret "shall reward thee openly", which shows God's response to our prayers; it's not just that God is *willing*, but that He *will* reward our secret prayers.

It's not for us to worry about how God's sovereignty affects our prayers; we are to pray believing the LORD hears prayer, is willing to respond to prayer, and can answer prayer depending on what and how we ask Him (Matthew 6:9-13; Luke 11:1-4; Matthew 7:7-11; Luke 11:5-13; Luke 18:1-5; Hebrews 11:6; 1 Timothy 2:8; Ephesians 6:18; Philippians 4:6-7; James 1:5-8; James 4:3; James 5:16-18; Jude 1:20; 1 John 5:14-15).

The beauty of prayer is this — God's response to our prayers will always fit within His predetermined purposes anyway. This is why no man has ever changed His mind; if God changed course in response to prayer, it was something He was already going to do anyway (Genesis 18:16-33; Exodus 32:7-14; Jonah 3). When God answers our prayers, it is because He was always intending to do so, and if our prayers go unanswered, it shows His unwillingness for the time they go unanswered (Luke 22:41-44). R.C. Sproul said it one way:

"Does prayer change God's mind?" My answer brought storms of protest. I said simply, "No." Now, if the person had asked me, "Does prayer change things?" I would have answered, "Of course!" - **R.C. Sproul**

Prayer is not overcoming God's reluctance. It is laying hold of His willingness. - **Martin Luther (attributed quote)**

Prayer is the means by which God changes things; we shouldn't forsake it just because God is sovereign. It doesn't matter what He is going to do, it doesn't matter that He already knows what we're to say — God invites Christians as sons and daughters to approach the throne of grace, and make their petitions, requests, sins, and dependence known in their prayers (Hebrews 4:16).

And in God being sovereign, He already knows *what* we need *when* we need it *before* we ask (Matthew 6:8), even though we may not know exactly what to ask for (Romans 8:26-27), or may not get what we *think* we need from God. As we pray, the omniscient God knows what we need, and He is willing to provide it (Matthew 6:31-33; Matthew 7:9-11).

> Bless the LORD, O my soul: and all that is within me, *bless* his holy name. <u>Bless the LORD, O my soul, and forget not all his benefits:</u> Who forgiveth all thine iniquities; who healeth all thy diseases; Who redeemeth thy life from destruction; who crowneth thee with lovingkindness and tender mercies; Who satisfieth thy mouth with good *things; so that* thy youth is renewed like the eagle's. - **Psalm 103:1-5 (KJV)**

Outside of our prayers being answered, there are many great benefits to being obedient to the call of prayer. Prayer aligns our will to the will of God (Matthew 6:10; Luke 11:2; Luke 22:42; Romans 12:1-2). Prayer allows us to display our understanding of God's Word, and make requests that are in biblical alignment with His will, so that we may be heard, and not ask amiss (1 John 5:14-15; James 4:3).

Prayer allows us to bear the blackness of our sins and wretched state before God in ways that no man could bear (1 John 1:8-9; Psalm 32:1-6; Proverbs 28:13; Psalm 51:1-14; Psalm 38:18). Prayer is the means where we draw on God's strength to overcome our flesh, the world, and Satan (Matthew 26:41; Romans 8:13-14; Isaiah 40:31; Psalm 91:1; James 4:7; Ephesians 6:10-18; 1 Peter 5:8-10; 1 John 2:15-17). Prayer emboldens us to overcome our fears (Daniel 6:10; Luke 12:4-5; Romans 8:31-39; Psalm 27:1; Isaiah 41:10; 1 John 4:16-18; 1 Samuel 17:40-54; 2 Kings 23:1-27; Joshua 1:1-9; Acts 4:31).

Prayer is where we are able to find peace in God during the turbulent storms of life (Luke 22:44; Philippians 4:6-7; 1 Peter 5:6-7; Isaiah 26:3-4; John 14:27; Mark 4:35-41; Psalm 34:17,

19). Prayer allows us to cultivate a persistent dependence upon God and the truth in His Word (Isaiah 40:31; Psalm 27:14; Lamentations 3:24-26; James 1:2-4; Psalm 130:2-7; Psalm 33:20-22; Psalm 118:8-9; Proverbs 3:5-8; Psalm 37:7-11; Psalm 46:10; Psalm 23; 2 Corinthians 12:7-10; Philippians 4:19).

Prayer is one of the ways we are actively filled with the Spirit, to where we do not quench the Spirit, or gratify the lusts of the flesh (Ephesians 5:17-20; 1 Thessalonians 5:19; Galatians 5:16-25; Ephesians 4:30; Job 32:18-20; John 7:38-39). Prayer puts us under spiritual strain and labour, so we can further exercise ourselves unto godliness (1 Timothy 4:7-10; Jude 1:20; 1 Corinthians 9:24-27; 1 Timothy 6:11-12; 2 Timothy 4:6-8; Hebrews 12:1-11).

Prayer is the furnace of God's secret place, where we are refined like silver and gold, and are conformed more and more into image and likeness of Christ, for even Jesus prayed (Psalm 66:10; Zechariah 13:9; 1 Peter 1:6-8; Revelation 3:18-19; Romans 8:29; Matthew 14:22-23; Mark 1:35; Mark 6:45-46; Luke 5:16; Luke 6:12; Matthew 26:36-42; Mark 14:32-39; Luke 22:39-44; Hebrews 5:7-9). Prayer deepens our affection and allegiance to God and His commands (Psalm 119:32; John 6:66-69; John 14:15, 21; Psalm 63:1-8). Prayer is where we have the opportunity to see God do exceeding abundantly above all that we ask or think (Ephesians 3:20; John 6:8-14).

Lastly, prayer is where we begin to delight in God all the more, and where we delight in Him, therein is He glorified (Proverbs 15:8; Psalm 141:1-2; Revelation 5:8; Revelation 8:3-4; Genesis 8:20-22; 1 Corinthians 10:31; 1 Samuel 15:22; 2 Chronicles 5:11-14; Psalm 50:14-15; John 14:13-14; Psalm 37:4; Psalm 147:11; Psalm 70:4; 3 John 1:4; Psalm 119:16, 35, 47, 77, 174). Like preaching, prayer works much good in us. In love, God invites us to pray to draw on Him and the manifold blessings He provides through prayer (Psalm 34:8-10).

CHAPTER 3 - THREE GOOD DOCTRINES YOU NEED FOR EVIL (PART 2)

In our fifth application of man's responsibility, all Christians have a call to live holy, and bear fruit. Jesus encapsulates this concept when speaking to His disciples:

> I am the true vine, and my Father is the husbandman. Every branch in me that beareth not fruit he taketh away: <u>and every *branch* that beareth fruit, he purgeth it, that it may bring forth more fruit. Now ye are clean through the word which I have spoken unto you. Abide in me, and I in you. As the branch cannot bear fruit of itself, except it abide in the vine; no more can ye, except ye abide in me. I am the vine, ye *are* the branches: He that abideth in me, and I in him, the same bringeth forth much fruit: for without me ye can do nothing.</u> If a man abide not in me, he is cast forth as a branch, and is withered; and men gather them, and cast *them* into the fire, and they are burned. If ye abide in me, and my words abide in you, ye shall ask what ye will, and it shall be done unto you. <u>Herein is my Father glorified, that ye bear much fruit; so shall ye be my disciples.</u> - **John 15:1-8 (KJV)**

What does it *mean* to bear fruit? It is walking in obedience to Scripture by the Spirit's power, which produces holiness in us to God's glory (John 17:17; Ephesians 5:25-27; John 4:23-24; Romans 8:14; Galatians 5:22-25; Romans 12:1-2; 1 Peter 1:22; Psalm 119:1-4, 9-11, 133; 2 Peter 1:2-8; John 14:15; Leviticus 20:7-8; 1 Peter 1:13-16; Leviticus 11:44-45; 2 Corinthians 7:1; Colossians 1:9-12; Hebrews 13:20-21). In all that we do, we do to the glory of God with the Bible as our authoritative guide:

> <u>All scripture *is* given by inspiration of God, and *is* profitable for doctrine, for reproof, for correction, for instruction in righteousness: That the man of God may be</u>

perfect, throughly furnished unto all good works. - 2 Timothy 3:16-17 (KJV)

I won't get into the myriad of ways in which we can bear fruit, but bearing fruit is the product of obedience and holiness, and holiness is shaped and cultivated by how we live, and we are actively responsible in pursuing it (2 Peter 3:13-14; 1 Thessalonians 5:23; 1 Peter 2:11-12; 1 Timothy 4:12-16; 2 Timothy 2:19-22; Philippians 2:14-16; James 1:27; 1 Thessalonians 4:1-8; 1 Chronicles 22:19; Psalm 119:57-60; Colossians 3:1-17; 1 Chronicles 16:29; Psalm 96:8-9). This is our sanctification, for no Christian becomes holy by accident:

> No man ever became holy by chance. There must be a resolve, a desire, a panting, a pining after obedience to God, or else we shall never have it. Set your heart, then, to seek the Lord your God. - **Charles H. Spurgeon**

If we do not pursue holiness, we will not become holy, and if we are slack in pursuing it, we will abound in sin and corruption, and fail to bear much fruit, let alone any fruit at all, for pursuing holiness is abiding in God (John 15:4-5, 7). If we sever ourselves from holiness, and do not bear fruit, we may be marked as unprofitable for the Master's use, and cast away from the fruit-bearing Vine, where we wither and are thrown into the fire of spiritual impotence [a lack of God-glorifying influence in this world] (John 15:6; Matthew 21:18-20; Revelation 2:4-5).

If we bear any fruit at all, God — the husbandman — will see to it that we will be prepared to bear more fruit (John 15:2). Holiness begets holiness (James 4:8; 2 Corinthians 6:14-18; Psalm 93:5; John 2:13-17; Hebrews 12:14; 1 John 3:3). Moreover, the fruit we bear is not simply for our spiritual aesthetic and decoration; our fruit is not only for us to "look the part" as Christians, for fruit wasn't designed to only look pleasant to the eye — the core purpose of fruit is to bless those who partake in its contents (Psalm 104:13-15; Genesis 2:8-9).

> <u>Ye are the salt of the earth: but if the salt have lost his savour, wherewith shall it be salted?</u> it is thenceforth good for nothing, but to be cast out, and to be trodden under foot of men. <u>Ye are the light of the world. A city that is set on an hill cannot be hid.</u> Neither do men light a candle, and put it under a bushel, <u>but on a candlestick; and it giveth light unto all that are in the house. Let your light so shine before men, that they may see your good works, and glorify your Father which is in heaven.</u> - **Matthew 5:13-16 (KJV)**

When we pursue obedience and holiness in our inner man, in our private life, in our marriages, among our family and friends, in our church and community, on our jobs, and in the public square, we will bear fruit and affect those environments. Holiness will even cause the secular man to acknowledge God, which is the very thing he suppresses; our holinesss will bring it to the surface (Genesis 41:38-41; Daniel 2:46-49; Daniel 3:24-30; John 2:6-11; Matthew 27:54; Mark 15:39; Luke 23:47).

Answering the call to be holy is our responsibility; we must take it upon ourselves to bear fruit. Only then will our salt retain its savour; only then will our light shine, and amplify its brightness before the world:

> But the path of the just *is* as the shining light, that shineth more and more unto the perfect day. - **Proverbs 4:18 (KJV)**

Yes, the LORD has sovereignly ordained good works for us to

walk in (Ephesians 2:10), yet at the same time, in this transcendent harmony, we are responsible for the fruit we bear. Inversely, we are also responsible for the fruit we *fail* to bear. For there will come a day where we'll all have to stand before the holy God, and give an account on what we did and what we failed to do. The Apostle Paul makes this known to Christians in a particular way:

> Wherefore we labour, that, whether present or absent, we may be accepted of him. For we must all appear before the judgment seat of Christ; that every one may receive the things *done* in *his* body, according to that he hath done, whether *it be* good or bad. - **2 Corinthians 5:9-10 (KJV)**

Even as Christians, God is not mocked; even though we have eternal life, we can't live any way we want to in this life, for one day, each and every Christian will appear before the judgment seat of Christ, where our works will be assessed and our words will be accounted for (1 Corinthians 3:9-15; Matthew 12:36).

This judgment is not unto condemnation for Christians; this judgment is an assessment our works and faithfulness on the Lord's behalf as His ambassadors, and it will result in our eternal rewards (Matthew 6:19-21). Therefore, how we live carries eternal implications, and it should cause us to eagerly await and reverentially fear that day.

Christian, let us not be ashamed, but have assurance on that day (Philippians 1:20; 2 Timothy 2:15; 1 John 2:28-29; 1 John 3:18-19). Let our hearts commend us in that we gave it all we had; we poured ourselves out as drink offerings in good works to God's glory (2 Timothy 4:6). When all is said and done, none of us will ever regret being more holy, labouring for the kingdom of God, and bearing fruit to God's glory (1 Corinthians 15:58; Galatians 6:7-10). By God's grace, be holy.

CHAPTER 3 - THREE GOOD DOCTRINES YOU NEED FOR EVIL (PART 2)

> The whole genius of the Christian religion runneth in this strain, to make men good and holy, and to breed the most excellent and choicest spirits that ever the world was blest with, and that it may be known that the life of faith is the most noble and powerful principle in the world. - **Thomas Manton**

> Be ye therefore perfect, even as your Father which is in heaven is perfect. - **Matthew 5:48 (KJV)**

The final application of man's responsibility ties into the very first one mentioned, but I couldn't leave it out. All men are responsible in the call to obey Scripture. The Bible does not only apply to Christians, but it applies to all men. If a man sins, but has never read the Bible, he is still guilty of sin; ignorance of God's law is no excuse:

> <u>And if a soul sin,</u> and commit any of these things which are forbidden to be done by the commandments of the LORD; <u>though he wist *it* not, yet is he guilty, and shall bear his iniquity</u>... It *is* a trespass offering: <u>he hath certainly trespassed against the LORD.</u> - **Leviticus 5:17, 19 (KJV)**

Scripture is binding upon all men, and all men are beholden to obey it, whether we are aware or ignorant of its contents. This doesn't only pertain to sins, but every demand and command according to God's design is binding upon a man, and is counted against him if he fails to obey it:

> If ye fulfil the royal law according to the scripture, Thou shalt love thy neighbour as thyself, ye do well: But if ye have respect to persons, ye commit sin, and are convinced of the law as transgressors. <u>For whosoever shall keep the</u>

> whole law, and yet offend in one *point*, he is guilty of all. For he that said, Do not commit adultery, said also, Do not kill. Now if thou commit no adultery, yet if thou kill, thou art become a transgressor of the law. - **James 2:8-11 (KJV)**

Not only is a man guilty of his sin, but he will reap the wages of his sin:

> For the wages of sin *is* death; but the gift of God *is* eternal life through Jesus Christ our Lord. - **Romans 6:23 (KJV)**

> Be not deceived; God is not mocked: for whatsoever a man soweth, that shall he also reap. For he that soweth to his flesh shall of the flesh reap corruption; but he that soweth to the Spirit shall of the Spirit reap life everlasting. - **Galatians 6:7-8 (KJV)**

This is why it is imperative for us to know the truth, hear the truth, practice the truth, and profess the truth, for the truth will free ourselves and others from the bondage of sin:

> And ye shall know the truth, and the truth shall make you free. - **John 8:32 (KJV)**

> Brethren, if any of you do err from the truth, and one convert him; Let him know, that he which converteth the sinner from the error of his way shall save a soul from death, and shall hide a multitude of sins. - **James 5:19-20 (KJV)**

And there you have it. We made it through the second doctrine we need for understanding evil. Man's responsibility is the antidote which neutralizes the poison pill of God's sovereignty.

CHAPTER 3 - THREE GOOD DOCTRINES YOU NEED FOR EVIL (PART 2)

It keeps us balanced in biblical orthodoxy (sound doctrine) and biblical orthopraxy (right conduct, right practice, right living). God will be sovereign as He is sovereign, and as He exercises His absolute sovereignty, we must exercise our responsibility to be obedient, faithful, zealous and fruitful for His glory, and for our ultimate good through the abundant life He provides (John 10:10; Philippians 2:12-13; 1 Timothy 4:6-16; 2 Corinthians 3:17-18).

We have one more doctrine to cover, and we will have fully scaled the mountains of biblical truth. We are in the final stretch of our ascent. I'm sure this theological climb has been arduous and humbling. Some readers might have become offended by the truth, and decided to turn back. Some readers may have felt that this journey was not worth the effort, and in their weariness, gave up on reaching the summit.

But for the Christian reader who pressed onwards and upwards despite offence, and despite the temptation to resign prematurely, I believe we will be blessed with a renewed spiritual perspective, be left in greater awe of God and His Word, and possess a firm foundation of doctrine that will help us to understand evil. I said it in the first chapter, and I'm saying it now. Let us reach the mountaintop together.

GOD'S PREEMINENT PURPOSE FOR CREATION

Man's chief aim is to glorify God (Isaiah 43:7; Psalm 86:12; 1 Peter 4:11; 1 Corinthians 10:31; Psalm 145; Psalm 148:11-13; John 17:9-11). God's chief aim is to glorify Himself. I *cannot* stress this enough. If you cannot understand this truth, you will have a very hard time embracing the subsequent arguments presented in this book; your journey to the mountaintop will end here. God's chief aim is to glorify Himself.

God is *too* God, and if we're honest, some of us may have a problem with that, because sometimes, we want God to be God in the ways *we* have perceived Him to be, not in the way that He *actually* is. We might falsely believe that God's preeminent purpose is to redeem us, and focus all of His efforts to attending to our good; we might conflate being the apple of God's eye as being the center of His universe, but this is not true. We might presume that since God is willing to freely give us all things, we are the end point of which all things are to serve or benefit. But this is a great error, because it inclines itself into man-centric theology, which is far from what the Bible teaches.

In reality, God's preeminent purpose is His glory. God's essential aim revolves around Him at the center. From Him, and through Him, and to Him are all things (Romans 11:36). Everything works in service to Him, namely His glory first and foremost, with our good being a secondary byproduct (Romans 8:28). Our ultimate good is linked, but secondary, to God's preeeminent purpose (Isaiah 43:25).

If you think I'm exaggerating, you will soon find that the LORD does not play about His glory; in fact, God righteously covets His glory, because all glory belongs to Him:

For of him, and through him, and to him, *are* all things: to whom *be* glory for ever. Amen. - **Romans 11:36 (KJV)**

Now unto the King eternal, immortal, invisible, the only wise God, *be* honour and glory for ever and ever. Amen. - **1 Timothy 1:17 (KJV)**

Unto him *be* glory in the church by Christ Jesus throughout all ages, world without end. Amen. - **Ephesians 3:21 (KJV)**

To God only wise, *be* glory through Jesus Christ for ever. Amen. - **Romans 16:27 (KJV)**

CHAPTER 3 - THREE GOOD DOCTRINES YOU NEED FOR EVIL (PART 2)

<u>Now unto God and our Father *be* glory for ever and ever. Amen.</u> - **Philippians 4:20 (KJV)**

But grow in grace, and *in* the knowledge of our Lord and Saviour Jesus Christ. <u>To him *be* glory both now and for ever. Amen.</u> - **2 Peter 3:18 (KJV)**

Make you perfect in every good work to do his will, working in you that which is wellpleasing in his sight, <u>through Jesus Christ; to whom *be* glory for ever and ever. Amen.</u> - **Hebrews 13:21 (KJV)**

<u>To the only wise God our Saviour, *be* glory and majesty, dominion and power, both now and ever. Amen.</u> - **Jude 1:25 (KJV)**

<u>To whom *be* glory for ever and ever. Amen.</u> - **Galatians 1:5 (KJV)**

And the Lord shall deliver me from every evil work, and will preserve *me* unto his heavenly kingdom: <u>to whom *be* glory for ever and ever. Amen.</u> - **2 Timothy 4:18 (KJV)**

<u>To him *be* glory and dominion for ever and ever. Amen.</u> - **1 Peter 5:11 (KJV)**

<u>Give unto the LORD the glory due unto his name; worship the LORD in the beauty of holiness.</u> - **Psalm 29:2 (KJV)**

Through Scripture, the Holy Spirit speaketh expressly — God wants every dreg and drop of glory to be ascribed to Him; no man, creature, or thing has a rightful claim to glory, for no one else is worthy of it. Only God is worthy of glory:

> Thou art worthy, O Lord, to receive glory and honour and power: for thou hast created all things, and for thy pleasure they are and were created. - **Revelation 4:11 (KJV)**

When we try to take glory for ourselves, God becomes magnificiently territorial, and the Lion of Judah will bear His fangs at us. We see this with Nebuchadnezzar, the king of Babylon; despite being warned of Daniel (Daniel 4:19-27), there came a day when Nebuchadnezzar credited himself as being the reason for Babylon's might, power, and majesty as a kingdom. He gloried in himself, not in God who gave him the kingdom to rule (Daniel 5:18-19; Jeremiah 27:4-8).

The Bible tells us that "while the word was in the king's mouth", God told Nebuchadnezzar that he would no longer rule Babylon, but would become like a beast and live among the beasts for seven years (Daniel 4:31-33). After seven years, Nebuchadnezzar came to his senses, and recognized to whom the glory belonged:

> And at the end of the days I Nebuchadnezzar lifted up mine eyes unto heaven, and mine understanding returned unto me, and I blessed the most High, and I praised and honoured him that liveth for ever, whose dominion *is* an everlasting dominion, and his kingdom *is* from generation to generation: Now I Nebuchadnezzar praise and extol and honour the King of heaven, all whose works *are* truth, and his ways judgment: and those that walk in pride he is able to abase. - **Daniel 4:34, 37 (KJV)**

God would not share His glory, and it took the deposed king of Babylon seven years to realize this (Daniel 5:20-21). Another stark example is King Herod. After delivering a speech, the people worshipped him as a god, and he accepted this false worship. Displeased by this, the LORD immediately smote Herod, and he was eaten up by worms and died because "he gave not God the glory" (Acts 12:23). No glory to us, all glory to Him (Psalm 115:1). God will not share His glory with anyone or anything (Isaiah 42:8; Isaiah 48:11). Do not contend with God for it, for we will lose that battle every time. The only way we are permitted to glory is not to glory in ourselves, but glory in God alone:

> Thus saith the LORD, Let not the wise *man* glory in his wisdom, neither let the mighty *man* glory in his might, let not the rich *man* glory in his riches: <u>But let him that glorieth glory in this, that he understandeth and knoweth me, that I *am* the LORD which exercise lovingkindness, judgment, and righteousness, in the earth: for in these *things* I delight, saith the LORD.</u> - **Jeremiah 9:23-24 (KJV)**

> That, according as it is written, <u>He that glorieth, let him glory in the Lord.</u> - **1 Corinthians 1:31 (KJV)**

> But he that glorieth, let him glory in the Lord. - **2 Corinthians 10:17 (KJV)**

God does all things for His glory. All of creation was made for God's glory (Revelation 4:11; Genesis 1:1). God did not create the heavens and the earth because He was lacking something, and needed creation to fulfill that need (Acts 17:24-25; Psalm 50:12; Exodus 3:14), but God *wanted* to create the universe for His own pleasure and glory.

God will go to great lengths to secure the glory ascribed for Him. God raised Pharaoh up and made Egypt prosperous, only to destroy Pharoah and ravage the nation, so that He would be glorified in all the earth through Israel's deliverance (Romans

9:17; Exodus 6:6-7; Exodus 7:5; Exodus 10:7; Exodus 12:12; Exodus 14:4, 17-18; Exodus 15:11-19; Psalm 106:7-8). God sought His glory first; Israel's deliverance was the byproduct of the glorious working of God's mighty hand in Egypt (Exodus 3:19-20). If you can recall from the last chapter, the whole reason for the doctrine of election is for God to showcase the glory of His full character — glory which God in His wisdom felt wouldn't be shown if He saved everyone, and did not have vessels of mercy and vessels of wrath (Romans 9:18-24; Ephesians 1:1-14).

God will even subject man to adverse circumstances so that He will be glorified. Job is a very good example of this. Maybe Job is aware of this in heaven, but while on earth, Job did not understand why his suffering started in the first place, but it was rooted in God's glory:

> And the LORD said unto Satan, Hast thou considered my servant Job, that *there is* none like him in the earth, a perfect and an upright man, one that feareth God, and escheweth evil? - **Job 1:8 (KJV)**

Remember that God brought Job to Satan's attention; Satan was minding his own business among the sons of God, and the LORD put the focus on Job. God wanted to highlight Job's righteousness, for Job's righteousness was worship unto God; his life was a sweet incense through which He would glory, for when we live right and according to God's design, God is glorified. Hearing this would be an affront to Satan — the spiritual ancestor of sin and rebellion — and stir something within the devil. The omniscient God knew where this was going:

Then Satan answered the LORD, and said, Doth Job fear

CHAPTER 3 - THREE GOOD DOCTRINES YOU NEED FOR EVIL (PART 2)

<u>God for nought? Hast not thou made an hedge about him, and about his house, and about all that he hath on every side? thou hast blessed the work of his hands, and his substance is increased in the land. But put forth thine hand now, and touch all that he hath, and he will curse thee to thy face.</u> - **Job 1:9-11 (KJV)**

Satan speaks directly about Job and in subtle subtext about God. Satan believes Job only serves God because of the protection and possessions He has provided to him, but if those things were taken away, Job would have no reason to serve the Lord, and even curse God to His face in contempt defiance.

What Satan is saying here is, "Job has a reason to serve you because of what you've given him, not because of who you are. You have fickle servants because you are a fickle God; beyond what you provide, you are not worthy of worship." So this wasn't just a *direct* indictment on Job's character, but it was also an *indirect* indictment on God's character, for when God's men sin and walk in rebellion, it gives the wicked boldness to blaspheme the name of the Lord for the conduct of His people, for the people ought to be a reflection of the King they serve (Isaiah 48:9-11; Ezekiel 20:13-14; Ezekiel 36:22-23).

God would not allow Satan to get away with these allegations against Him and Job, nor would He allow His name to be profaned through Job's life, so for the glory of His name, God sought to prove Satan a liar, and put Job's faith to the test:

<u>And the Lord said unto Satan, Behold, all that he hath *is* in thy power; only upon himself put not forth thine hand.</u> So Satan went forth from the presence of the Lord. - **Job 1:12 (KJV)**

God subjected Job to great suffering — he lost his livestock, his servants, all of his children, his physical wellness, and his reputation among men, but Job retained his faith and integrity in God (Job 1:20-22; Job 2:9-10). Job's suffering was primarily intended to vindicate God before Satan, and the LORD sacrificed Job's well-being for a season to do it. God first sought to be glorified from Job's trial (Job 2:3).

For His glory, the LORD used Job to prove what kind of God He is. He showed Satan — and us — that the faith He gave to Job was greater than the wealth He gave to him, and that same faith would sustain Job in his loss and sufferings, even though Job pondered his ways, was perplexed, and did not understand what God was doing. This exercise of faith was for God's glory.

Thankfully, Job's trial was not only *for* God's glory, but worked *to* God's glory in multiple ways. First, Job's suffering was used to refine his faith, and give him a better perspective on the God he served; his pain caused him to know the LORD in a more visceral and intimate way:

> <u>I have heard of thee by the hearing of the ear: but now mine eye seeth thee.</u> Wherefore I abhor *myself*, and repent in dust and ashes. - **Job 42:5-6 (KJV)**

God used the trial to expose Job's self-righteousness (Job 32:1-2; Job 33:1-13), and made Job a better man than he was had he not underwent his sufferings (Job 23:10). Secondly, Job's suffering was used to refine *our* faith. As Job was lamenting, he would have probably never guessed that his trial would be recorded:

> <u>Oh that my words were now written! oh that they were printed in a book!</u> That they were graven with an iron pen and lead in the rock for ever! - **Job 19:23-24 (KJV)**

CHAPTER 3 - THREE GOOD DOCTRINES YOU NEED FOR EVIL (PART 2)

The LORD turned Job's grieving wishes into a reality, and gave him his own book in the Bible, engraved with the eternal finger of God! God vindicated Job in more ways than one (Job 42:10-17). Through this book, Job became an example for us on how to respond to loss, suffer well under trial, lament and cry out to God, and trust in God's sovereignty and character by faith. We also learn that God is worthy of worship first because of who He is, not because of what He can give.

After God's glory and Job's eventual good, we are also encouraged and built up in our faith, for it was for our learning that these accounts were written in Scripture (Romans 15:4; Hebrews 12:1-3; James 5:10-11). In every facet, Job's adverse circumstances worked and continue to work to the glory of God.

Job is not our only example of this. Look at the man who was blind from birth; Jesus said it wasn't the man's sins, nor his parents' sins that caused him to be born blind, but he was born this way "that the works of God should be made manifest in him" (John 9:3). This man was subjected to a life of blindness all for the purpose of God getting the glory in restoring his sight (John 9:1-11). Christ allowed Lazarus to get sick and die for the glory of God, specifically for Christ to glorify Himself in raising Lazarus from the dead (John 11:1-6, 11, 40-46).

There is no better example than Jesus Himself — Christ's death was intended to glorify God (John 12:27-28; John 13:31-32; John 17:1). God's glory was the primary objective of Christ's death, with our salvation being purchased through this glorious event; in seeking His glory, God brought many sons to glory through Christ (Isaiah 53:10-11; Hebrews 2:9-13). God will subject man to adverse circumstances for His glory, and God will go to the greatest extremes for His glory. No one or nothing is off limits.

In light of this weighty truth, we might think God is sadistic because He is willing to subject us to pain for His glory; we might feel we shouldn't be subjected to this as God's creation, and this treatment is counterintuitive to a God who says He loves His children (1 John 3:1; Romans 5:8). It might even hurt our pride knowing we are essentially pawns for God's glory, which God can use as He likes to achieve His preeminent purpose.

First off, if you think God is sadistic, your human mind is carnal and debased (Romans 8:6-8); our God is thrice-holy, and there is no darkness in Him at all (1 John 1:5; Isaiah 6:1-5; Revelation 4:8). Furthermore, God has chosen to link His glory to our good (Romans 8:28). Through His preeminent purpose, Christians are able to experience the ultimate good in salvation. The LORD doesn't have to do this — God would be perfectly justified in seeking His glory alone, but thanks be to God that is not the case; our good is a secondary yet merciful byproduct of God's glory, even if it means subjecting us to hardship and chastening to bring this good about (Hebrews 12:5-11; Job 5:17-18; Psalm 138:8; Philippians 1:6; 1 Peter 5:10-11).

Finally, if it hurts our pride, good! There shouldn't be any pride to display before the Creator of heaven and earth. You might hate the idea of being a pawn for God's glory, but here is the deathblow to your gripe and grievance with God — we deserve nothing good from God. In all of the Bible, only one verse explicitly conveys this truth, and we are privileged to get it through the patriarch Jacob:

<u>I am not worthy of the least of all the mercies, and of all the truth, which thou hast shewed unto thy servant;</u> for with my staff I passed over this Jordan; and now I am become two bands. - **Genesis 32:10 (KJV)**

In his prayer to the LORD, Jacob recognized how God graciously

CHAPTER 3 - THREE GOOD DOCTRINES YOU NEED FOR EVIL (PART 2)

increased his wealth and his family from nothing, yet Jacob acknowledges that he deserves none of it; the wealth, the family, the deeper understanding of God that he's gained — these are mercies which go beyond what he actually deserves from God, which is no good thing. When we consider the word, "least" is the *minimum* portion next to nothing, and here Jacob is saying he is not even worthy of that. We deserve nothing good from God, and God does not owe us anything.

Christian, do you *truly* believe in your heart that you deserve nothing good from God? Or do you just say it as a soothing, but empty, religious platitude for Sunday morning? I would say that many of us would concede to the latter. Within Christian culture, we embed the phrase in our songs and Christian conversations with the brethren, but it is very hard to embrace the implication of this truth if it were applied to our lives. If we had everything taken away from us like Job, would we still whistle the same tune of deserving nothing good from God (Job 3:25; Job 13:15)?

Coincidentally, this eventually became Job's issue with God; at some point, Job believed his righteous living warranted better treatment from God — he felt that God's judgment was extreme, and believed he at least deserved to plead his innocence before God, or receive a reason for his affliction (Job 7:17-21; Job 9:14-35; Job 10:1-9; Job 13:3, 22-24; Job 16:21; Job 19:7-12; Job 21:4; Job 23:1-10; Job 27:1-2; Job 30:20-21; Job 31:2-6, 35-37). But God did not owe Job an audience, nor did the LORD owe Job an explanation for his affliction (Job 33:1-13), even though God knew He afflicted Job without cause (Job 2:3).

Outside of glorifying Himself, shaming Satan, and refining Job, God wanted to teach us one of the hardest lessons we will ever learn: Just because God is good does not mean He has to be good to you. If God did nothing good for you going forward, nothing about God would change. His goodness would not diminish one bit (Psalm 100:5; Psalm 107:8, 15, 21, 31; Psalm 135:3). Think about it — if we don't deserve anything good from God, why does He have to be good to us in the first place? All the mercies we've enjoyed from God were mercies we never deserved to begin with, so we should not contend with God if they are taken away (easier said than done, I know).

The LORD wanted to drive this point home with Job; through his affliction, God was essentially communicating to us, "Look at Job — he is the pinnacle of a righteous man in his best state, but even this is altogether vanity. I will do with him as I please for my glory." Again, not sadism, but the righteous and sovereign God doing what He wants with His own (Matthew 20:15).

This brought great conflict within Job's soul. He felt his righteous living shouldn't have led to this affliction. But his righteousness did not make him beyond reproach with God, because like all of us, Job truly deserved nothing good from God (Psalm 130:3; Job 34:23).

Righteousness may *position* you for the good things of God, but it does not *entitle* you to the good things of God. By righteousness, I'm speaking about that practical righteousness that aims to align with God's law and walk in His ways, not the righteousness of Christ. Obviously, in Christ, we are entitled to a great deal of many spiritual blessings and heavenly riches (Ephesians 1:3). That is not what I'm talking about. Whatever is given to us can be taken away, regardless of how righteous we are. Righteousness is to our benefit, and we don't seek the LORD in vain (Job 34:7-12; Job 35:1-9; Hebrews 11:32-40).

These hard sayings shouldn't simply take residence in our minds, but should be etched upon our hearts. How humble we would become! How much more glorious would God's mercies appear! If God has been good to you at all, it is because He has chosen to be abundantly merciful to you (Psalm 145:9; Exodus 34:6-7; 1 Chronicles 16:34; Psalm 106:1; Ephesians 2:4-7). No matter what we gain or lose, we were made for God's glory, so let us live unto that end (Ecclesiastes 12:13). We thank God for being a merciful God and the mercies He's bestowed, because we don't deserve any of it (Lamentations 3:22-26; Matthew 8:8; Luke 7:6-7; Matthew 15:21-28; Matthew 9:27-30; Mark 10:46-52; Psalm 37:26; Psalm 62:12; Psalm 86:5; Psalm 86:13; Psalm 86:15; Psalm 103:8; Psalm 103:17; Psalm 116:5; Psalm 145:8; Luke 18:13; Micah 7:18; Hebrews 8:10-12).

> We are hell-deserving creatures. If we are not humble we ought to be. - **Charles H. Spurgeon**

In principle, God owes us nothing, and we all deserve hell as children of wrath (Ephesians 2:1-3; John 3:36; Romans 1:18). Strictly speaking, the only thing God owes us are the things He's committed to give us that have been prescribed in His Word — not because we've done something to earn these things, but because He Himself has graciously committed it to us. Speaking of which, there is one more way that God pursues His preeminent purpose, and seeks to glorify Himself. We learn of this way in the verse below:

> I will worship toward thy holy temple, and praise thy name for thy lovingkindness and for thy truth: <u>for thou hast magnified thy word above all thy name.</u> - **Psalm 138:2 (KJV)**

This is one of the best verses in Scripture to showcase God's glory. God has magnified His word *above* His name. What does this even mean? Well, God's "word" are the words that have proceeded from His mouth or have been etched by His finger, and have been perfectly distilled in the form of inspired Scripture, which we now have in the Bible. So God has magnified Scripture above His name. Now in this verse, to "magnify" comes from the Hebrew word *gādal*, meaning to "make great", to make high, to lift up, to make much of, and to value highly.

God has lifted up Scripture above His name. Lastly, "thy name" is not simply a reference to God's names such as JEHOVAH, God, or the LORD, but in the context of the Bible, a "name" is intended to encapsulate everything associated with a person — it captures who a person is, including all that they have ever done. So when God says He has magnified His word above His name, God is saying that He has esteemed Scripture above His very Person. While God is the highest Being, He has willingly subjected Himself to the word He has spoken. Why would God do this? Because God seeks His glory.

By magnifying His word above His name, this in itself creates a positive feedback loop to God's glory, for God will get glory for upholding every jot and tittle in His eternal Word (Matthew 5:18; Luke 16:17); it speaks volumes to His character and majesty. God stakes His very character on the line — if any iota or scintilla of His word fails, then He ceases to be the God He proclaims to be, for He has failed in upholding His word, which He said He always would do (Isaiah 55:11; Joshua 23:14-16), which would then make the God who cannot lie a liar.

But since our God is glorious, He stakes His very character on fulfilling His word because He *knows* He will perform every word. Christian, outside of the God-Man Jesus Christ, there is no man you know that has fully kept his word every, single time throughout his life. At some point, whether by choice, circumstance or human limitation, we have all failed in doing the thing we said we would do. But not our God. Look at the infinite chasm of virtue between us and our Maker. For this alone, God should be praised. For this alone, God should be glorified. Keeping His promises and fulfilling His word is another way the Lord glorifies Himself (Isaiah 42:21).

Of all that God has promised, not one syllable shall ever fail. - **Charles H. Spurgeon**

A FIRM FOUNDATION

Here, we've reached the end — three good doctrines you need to understand evil. God is absolutely sovereign. Man is absolutely responsible. God seeks His glory above all else. These doctrines will serve as the bedrock that will establish you theologically, and guide your understanding going forward, for a three-stranded cord is not easily broken (Ecclesiastes 4:12).

At this point, some of you may already see how this all connects to the big picture of this book, and I hope that even though these doctrines are not explicitly mentioned, they will permeate throughout this book, and be quickly called to mind. We are standing on a firm foundation.

We made our descent into theological valleys. Did this break your pride and make you more humble? Were there any unbiblical misconceptions and presumptions you had no choice but to set aside? If so, praise God! As we made our humbling ascent, we were finally able to reach the proverbial mountaintop. What do you see from this vantage point? Have you gained a clearer spiritual perspective through studying biblical theology? Do you see the beauty of God's grace in full view? Are you now in greater awe of God and His Word? If so, praise God!

I pray that this book will bless and enrich the life of every Christian who reads it. With each page, I hope that the reality of this truth grows, and swells up within you until it becomes undeniable — our God is awesome.

I form the light, and create darkness: I make peace, and create evil: I the LORD do all these *things*.

ISAIAH 45:7 (KJV)

Whate'er my God ordains is right:
his holy will abideth;
I will be still, whate'er he doth,
and follow where he guideth.
He is my God; though dark my road,
he holds me that I shall not fall:
wherefore to him I leave it all.

Whate'er my God ordains is right:
he never will deceive me;
he leads me by the proper path;
I know he will not leave me.
I take, content, what he hath sent;
his hand can turn my griefs away,
and patiently I wait his day.

Whate'er my God ordains is right:
though now this cup, in drinking,
may bitter seem to my faint heart,
I take it, all unshrinking.
My God is true; each morn anew
sweet comfort yet shall fill my heart,
and pain and sorrow shall depart.

Whate'er my God ordains is right:
his holy will abideth;
I will be still, whate'er he doth,
and follow where he guideth.
He is my God; though dark my road,
he holds me that I shall not fall:
wherefore to him I leave it all.

Samuel Rodigast

CHAPTER 4
God Created Evil – A Biblical Argument

> I form the light, and create darkness: I make peace, and create evil: I the LORD do all these *things*.
> **Isaiah 45:7 (KJV)**

God created evil, but no one wants to give Him the credit. According to the Bible, God created evil, and though He created evil, God is still good. Evil showcases the goodness and purposes of God, while working towards the Christian's ultimate good. Evil was created for God's glory, and it is why He deserves the credit, for God Himself wants the credit for evil's creation. Evil is in good hands – in God's good hands. This is our thesis for this book.

As a quick refresher, when I define "evil", I'm referring to the concept of evil, the parameters of evil, and the forms and expressions of evil that have been outlined in the Bible. The concept, parameters, and the forms in which evil is expressed and manifest in our world were designed by God Himself. The reason it exists, and its ability to exist is because of God.

I've likened God's relationship with evil to an inventor going to a patent office. An inventor first comes up with an idea, then gives life to the idea with a tangible design; the designer outlines the blueprint, and defines their invention's purpose, functions and capabilities. Once the idea is properly fleshed out, and functions according the designer's intended purpose, the inventor goes to the patent office. The patent office is where you go to protect the ownership rights of your invention. By securing a patent, it bears record of the invention's connection to the designer.

God's creation of evil operates in the same way. God lays out the concept for evil; He maps out what it is, defines its purpose, designs how it will function and take form, and bears record of His invention through Scripture. The Bible is the patent office; Scripture gives God's concept of evil the stamp of approval, legitimizing God's authorship and rightful claim over the idea. If God doesn't draw up schematics and functional parameters for evil, evil could never be what it is.

Without God, evil would never reach the patent office; it could not be an idea supported by Scripture, nor would it be something that could be experienced by us in our present world, because evil wouldn't exist (Colossians 1:16-17). Therefore, any claims for God creating evil can only be legitimized with Scripture. I would not be able to support my position by any other measure.

I repeated this example verbatim from Chapter 1, and it bears repeating because Chapter 1 was over 100 pages ago, which means many of us have probably forgotten the core premise of this book, but this should bring us back up to speed. Now, if Scripture is the only way I can support God's legitimate claim for creating evil, then my arguments must begin with the Bible, particularly the Scripture which inspired this book in the first place — Isaiah 45:7.

Starting here, we will analyze this verse extensively, address the common arguments that refute the literal meaning of Isaiah 45:7, and use Scripture to debunk these rebuttals while reinforcing the explicit interpretation of the text. God created evil because He explicitly said so in Isaiah 45:7. Let's begin.

CHAPTER 4 - GOD CREATED EVIL – A BIBLICAL ARGUMENT

HATH GOD REALLY SAID?

Isaiah 45:7 says, "I form the light, and create darkness: I make peace, and create evil: I the LORD do all these *things*." Many Christians don't believe God would actually say such a thing, or believe that God literally meant what He said. That is why when this verse comes up, Christians and theologians start to engage in spiritual gymnastics to remove the literal meaning from this verse; they pull the potency out of God's words to comfort their own conscience, and become misguided apologists for God. But this is wrong, and God doesn't need that; He said what He said. One of the foundational rules of Bible study is God says what He means, and means what He says. So when God intends for Scripture to be taken literal, it must be taken literal in its proper context *first* before other interpretations and applications are gleaned from it.

When we read things literally, we can see that each of these phrases can be tied back to creation, and the creation account in Genesis must always be read as a literal account first (Hebrew 11:1; Psalm 33:6-9; Exodus 20:11). We know that God forms the light because He created light on the first day (Genesis 1:3-5). What I'm about to say next is very, very important. Please make a note of it in your minds. Continuing on with our literal exposition, God says He creates darkness. Interestingly enough, this is the very first time in the whole, entire Bible that the LORD explicitly acknowledges that He creates darkness. You will find God *dividing* the light from the darkness, but you will *not* find God *creating* darkness in the Genesis account.

Though their creation was not mentioned in Genesis, we know that the waters and darkness existed *before* the light was called into existence, and the first creation day was completed (Genesis 1:2). The mere fact that these things already existed allows us to rightfully presume – not wrongly speculate – they were created by God, for God created all things (Colossians 1:16; John 1:1-3). Again, their existence confirms they were created by God.

As a side note, Christians wrongly believe that darkness is simply the *absence* of light, or the *opposite* of light, and in a moral and symbolic sense, that is somewhat true (Job 30:26; Psalm 107:8-14; Proverbs 4:18-19; Ecclesiastes 2:13; Isaiah 5:20; Isaiah 9:2; Isaiah 42:5-7; Isaiah 50:10; Amos 5:18-20; Micah 7:8; Matthew 6:22-23; John 1:4-5; John 8:12; John 12:44-46; 2 Corinthians 4:6; 2 Corinthians 6:14; Ephesians 5:8; Colossians 1:12-13; 1 Thessalonians 5:4-5; 1 Peter 2:9; 1 John 1:5-7). But that is not *entirely* true according to Genesis 1.

We presume darkness is the absence or opposite of light because of how light relates to dark in our world and universe. But the Bible shows us that darkness preceded the light, is a created substance all on its own, and from the very beginning, darkness was never dependent on created light's presence or absence to exist. Instead of simply being the absence or opposite of light, God primarily designed darkness as its own essence to be the *contrast* to light (Genesis 1:4). This knowledge might come in handy later.

Moving on, God states He makes peace. You won't find the term "peace" in Genesis 1, but it was very much present and established in the six days of creation, for on the sixth day, God looked upon every thing He made in heaven and earth, and recognized that all of it was "very good" (Genesis 1:31). When it was made, all of creation was in a state of peace (or *shalom*) where all things coincided in literal, perfect harmony – God was at peace with His creation, and all aspects of creation were in harmony with each other. Peace was a facet and expression of creation's goodness. This state of peace and tranquility was literally disrupted when Adam sinned, which brought humanity and creation under a curse (Genesis 3:8-19; Romans 8:18-23).

CHAPTER 4 - GOD CREATED EVIL – A BIBLICAL ARGUMENT

So far, we are able to cite the literal, word-for-word meaning of the first three phrases in Isaiah 45:7. And now we get to God saying He creates evil. If all of the previous phrases are consistently referencing events at creation in a literal sense, why would we abandon the literal interpretation when God says He creates evil? That is inconsistent with the intent and pattern of this Scripture. So we must take God at His word, and believe He means what He says. We ought to interpret God creating evil with a literal meaning before we go anywhere else.

When we take His word at face value, the LORD says He literally creates evil. The word "evil" used here comes from the Hebrew word *ra'*, which primarily means the essence of moral sin and wickedness, but can also involve the concepts of calamity, misery, distress, adversity, injury and wrong depending on the context. The Hebrew word *ra'* occurs throughout the Old Testament, with its first mention being found in Genesis 2:9.

If we follow the intent and pattern of this Scripture, and reference each phrase back to the creation account in Genesis, then God is telling us that at some point, He designed evil. He designed evil as a concept, created the essence of moral sin and wickedness, established its functional parameters (how it operates), and determined all the forms and expressions of evil that could manifest in creation, which would ultimately flow out from evil's defined essence. Evil is designed by God, defined by God, and exists because of God according to Isaiah 45:7. That is the literal interpretation of the Scripture set before us.

To ensure you heard God right, the LORD caps off this bombshell of a verse by saying, "I the LORD do all these *things*." If you've been wondering where evil comes from, God is giving you the answer you've been searching for. Don't ignore what's right in front of you. Don't engage in spiritual gymnastics to explain the literal meaning of God's words away. God created evil, and He wants us to know it.

The reason why we reject what God is saying comes down to a problem we've had since Adam and Eve — we do not trust God at His word. We look at the literal words on the Bible's pages, and begin to contemplate, "Hath God really said?", and then we become bewildered trying to figure out where evil comes from, for we have forsaken the essential piece to this mysterious puzzle, primarily because we are unwilling to take God at His word. God says what He means, and means what He says.

As a concept and capacity that operates in creation, evil's invisible essence was created by God, for all things were created by God, including invisible things:

> <u>For by him were all things created, that are in heaven, and that are in earth, visible and invisible</u>, whether *they be* thrones, or dominions, or principalities, or powers: <u>all things were created by him, and for him: And he is before all things, and by him all things consist.</u> - **Colossians 1:16–17 (KJV)**

Outside of God, nothing can "be" without being "made". Outside of God, nothing can "consist" without being made to "exist". That includes invisible things like sin and evil. Is evil invisible? Yes, evil is invisible — we cannot visibly see evil's essence, we can't capture it out of thin air, nor can we tangibly hold it in our hands, or put it in a bottle. However, though evil's essence is invisible, its forms and expressions are visible in our world, for the essence is manifested through its expression.

What do I mean by this? Unless they are inherent to God's nature and attributes, conceptual things in our universe are *still* created things, even though their essence is invisible. Things like good, evil, love, hatred, faith, hope, peace, and joy, to name a few — these are invisible, conceptual things which have tangible expressions, and are things we are able to feel, experience, and express within the fabric of God's created universe. The quality of a thing is manifest in the thing that reflects it, even though the quality itself may not be visible or tangible. Evil is no different; its invisible essence is very much visible, and all of its expressions are derived from a moral concept that was created by God.

> All being, power, life, emotion, and perfection, are from God. - **Matthew Henry**

Based on Isaiah 45:7, God created evil, but Christendom has rejected the literal meaning of this verse, and offered their own rebuttals to refute this explicit interpretation. But are these theological rebuttals sufficient to dispel the controversy associated with this verse? We'll explore some of the most common counter-arguments that you may have — or may not have — heard of, and use Scripture to see if they actually hold any weight. I will try to address each argument in the order of weakest to strongest. At the end of it all, I believe the literal meaning of Isaiah 45:7 will stand under scrutiny, and we shall all see that "Man shall not live by bread alone, but by every word that proceedeth out of the mouth of God."

Argument 1 — You're Not Considering the Context

The first argument is I am only analyzing Isaiah 45:7 in a vacuum, and I am not considering the larger context wherein this verse is found. If I properly consider the larger context, then my understanding of this verse would change, and it would not lend itself to a literal interpretation.

To keep ourselves honest, what is the larger context? Well,

the larger context begins in Isaiah 44:28 and spills into Isaiah 45, where the LORD declares that He will raise up Cyrus, the king of Persia, to deliver the Israelites after 70 years of captivity in Babylon, and allow them to return to Jerusalem in Judah (Isaiah 44:28; Isaiah 45:1-6; Ezra 1:1-4; 2 Chronicles 36:20-23).

The apologists for this argument say once you consider the context, Isaiah 45:7 is a symbolic reference to Cyrus' exploits for Israel and against Babylon, and is *not* a direct reference to the creative acts of God. According to them, the "light" and "peace" used here refers to the liberation God would bring to Israel through Cyrus, while the contrasting "darkness" and "evil" refer to the judgment and calamity God would bring to Babylon through Cyrus. The statements in Isaiah 45:7 are not about the creative works of God, but they are about the symbolic outcomes the LORD would work in Cyrus through conquest and war. With greater context, the apologists in this camp conclude that Isaiah 45:7 should be limited to a symbolic interpretation, not a literal one.

When I survey the symbolic interpretation, I actually agree with it; I think from a symbolic standpoint, the statements of Isaiah 45:7 could have an application to Cyrus' exploits among the nations, but I still don't agree with the conclusion drawn from this argument, which is that a literal interpretation doesn't exist, and the phrases in Isaiah 45:7 *must* be constrained to a symbolic interpretation.

The problem here is even with greater context, it is more of a stretch to loosen our grip on the literal interpretation of the text to hold fast to a symbolic one, and prop it up as the one and only interpretation. When we do this, we begin to abandon good, biblical exegesis to adopt a faulty hermeneutic, which will ultimately hinder our efforts to rightly divide the word of truth (2 Timothy 2:15).

CHAPTER 4 - GOD CREATED EVIL – A BIBLICAL ARGUMENT

While Isaiah 45:7 *could* symbolically be talking about Cyrus, we *know* God is literally talking about Himself within this immediate context. Constraining this verse to only a symbolic interpretation is misguided, especially when an explicit interpretation is available to us. As we explore the larger context, we see that Isaiah 45:7 is not constrained by its context, but informed by its context, and can be understood literally without transforming its meaning:

> I *am* the LORD, and *there is* none else, *there is* no God beside me: I girded thee, though thou hast not known me: That they may know from the rising of the sun, and from the west, that *there is* none beside me. I *am* the LORD, and *there is* none else. I form the light, and create darkness: I make peace, and create evil: I the LORD do all these *things*. - **Isaiah 45:5-7 (KJV)**

Cyrus is referenced here, but these sections of the passage are not about him; here, we have moved from talking about Cyrus, and are now talking about God. God is revealing more of who He is within the context of foretelling His work through Cyrus. This is not a new occurrence in Scripture; throughout the Old Testament, God will randomly reveal facets of His nature and plans within various – and usually unrelated – contexts.

For example, within the context of making man on the sixth day, God revealed that He was a triune Being (Genesis 1:26; 1 John 5:7; Matthew 28:19). During the fall of man in Genesis 3, the LORD alluded to the future work of Christ, commonly known as the *protoevangelium* (Genesis 3:15). Prior to Adam and Eve being banished from the garden of Eden, God revealed He already possessed the knowledge of good and evil (Genesis 3:22). When Moses was called by God at the burning bush, God told Moses that He was the "I AM THAT I AM", which is the quintessential term that exemplifies God's self-existence and self-sufficiency, also known as God's aseity (Exodus 3:14; John 8:58). In promising deliverance for the Israelites in Egypt, the LORD also revealed to Moses that His name was "JEHOVAH", which is something God did not even reveal to Abraham, Isaac, or Jacob (Exodus 6:1-7; Psalm 83:18; Isaiah 12:2; Isaiah 26:4).

When Balaam blessed Israel for the third and final time, the LORD revealed that a Star and Sceptre (Jesus, the Messiah) would come out of Israel within this context (Numbers 24:15-18). As Moses issued warnings against divination to the Israelites, God decreed that He would one day raise up a Prophet (Jesus Christ) among them (Deuteronomy 18:9-19). There are probably more examples I haven't included, but this is all to show that God has always done this — at specific points within various contexts in Scripture, God chooses to reveal aspects of His nature and His doings. In these contexts, we learn something new about God through His revelations.

Isaiah 45:7 is no different. Yes, this verse is found within the context of Cyrus' future conquests, but within the context, it still reveals something to us about God. Here, we learn that like all created things in the universe, evil was also created by God. We should take God at His word, believe God literally means what He says, and should not impose a symbolic meaning on Isaiah 45:7 just because we question the implications of this statement, or are uncomfortable with the implications of this statement.

Argument 2 — "Evil" Means Something Else
The second argument is the word "evil" used in Isaiah 45:7 does not refer to the essence of moral sin and wickedness, but means "calamity", namely the calamity of bad outcomes and disasters in our world. In this context, the evil that God brings

about are calamities and disasters such as the global flood (Genesis 6), the decimation of Sodom and Gomorrah (Genesis 19:24-25), the ten plagues upon Egypt (Exodus 7-12), and any other ruinous judgment that God brings upon sinful men as a rightful application of His justice. As John Gill puts it, the evil described here is "not the evil of sin" but rather "the evil of punishment for sin, God's sore judgments, famine, pestilence, evil beasts, and the sword, or war... this usually is the effect of sin; may be sometimes lawfully engaged in; whether on a good or bad foundation is permitted by God; moreover, all afflictions, adversities, and calamities, come under this name, and are of God" (Job 2:10; Lamentations 3:37-40; Amos 3:6).

In summary, the evil used here is God simply executing judgment through the effects of sin, rather than creating the essence of sin and evil itself. The evil God creates are the negative outcomes He produces in response to sin; it is not something God actually made.

Like the first argument we explored, I agree with this argument as well; any time God is said to be doing evil in the Bible, it is never the evil of sin and moral wickedness, but the rightful application of His justice against sin, or His producing of bad outcomes in a sinful world. It is a transcendent and "morally good" evil that God alone wields; I define this as "the evil of bad outcomes", which we will explore in Chapter 5, and this is a consistent association with God doing evil in Scripture. That being said, Isaiah 45:7 should not be lazily pigeon-holed into this particular association God has with evil.

Isaiah 45:7 breaks away from this association for a few reasons. First off, in staying consistent with the literal interpretation from Argument 1, this is the only Scripture in all of the Bible which says God "creates" evil, which provides this verse with a unique distinction, and separates it from all the other verses that portray God exercising His righteous evil. We wrongly presume that the evil presented in Isaiah 45:7 fits in with the evil of bad outcomes, but creating evil's essence and expressions is *not* the same as the righteous evil God exercises in calamities, disasters, and afflictions.

Secondly, what further separates Isaiah 45:7 from the other associations is the pattern and intent of creation language used in the verse. As I've said before, the pattern of each statement in Isaiah 45:7 is first intended to redirect our minds back to creation. At creation, light was formed. At creation, darkness was created. At creation, peace was made.

But at creation, there was no "calamity" to be found; no calamity, disaster or bad outcome was rendered at creation, for everything the LORD made in heaven and earth was "very good" (Genesis 1:31). There was no reason for God to execute His righteous evil on sinful men, because after the six days of creation, there were no sinful men or creatures, for sin was not a part of the picture yet. So to say evil means "calamity" is inconsistent with the creation language intended for the verse. But if evil refers to creating the essence of moral sin and wickedness, then Isaiah 45:7 stays consistent with the pattern of creation language intended for the verse.

In this context, calamity does not properly capture the core essence of evil here, but even if I were to accept "calamity" as the appropriate definition, my argument would still be valid, and I can use an account in Scripture to prove it. In Luke 13, Jesus is preaching to the people, and He begins to provide insight on two tragedies, and shares insight about those who suffered those tragedies:

> There were present at that season some that told him of the Galilaeans, whose blood Pilate had mingled with their sacrifices. And Jesus answering said unto them, Suppose ye that these Galilaeans were sinners above all the Galilaeans,

because they suffered such things? <u>I tell you, Nay: but, except ye repent, ye shall all likewise perish.</u> Or those eighteen, upon whom the tower in Siloam fell, and slew them, think ye that they were sinners above all men that dwelt in Jerusalem? <u>I tell you, Nay: but, except ye repent, ye shall all likewise perish.</u> - **Luke 13:1-5 (KJV)**

Jesus teaches us a sobering lesson here. In the first tragedy, it seems that there were a group of Galilaeans who were unjustly killed by Pontius Pilate, and in a show of sacrilege, had the Galilaeans' own blood mixed with the blood of the sacrifices they offered up to God. Jesus reveals that the Galilaeans did not die because their sins were greater than anyone else's — they died because of the reality of sin and death in the world. Understanding this, Christ calls the people to repent so they don't die in their sins.

With the second tragedy, eighteen people died after a tower in Siloam fell on them. Jesus notes that the eighteen did not die because they were the greatest sinners in Jerusalem — they died because of the reality of sin and death in the world. Bringing attention to the real issue, Christ again calls the people to repent so they don't die in their sins.

What's my point? Well, we know in both of these tragedies, God was sovereign; these events would fall within the evil or calamities that God can bring about. Yet in each of these tragic scenarios, Jesus tells us that the most pressing need is not to grieve, or seek emotional healing for these disasters — the most pressing need is to repent of sin. Why would this be Christ's consistent conclusion? Because the evil of sin is the greatest calamity known to man. The people Jesus spoke to may not have died in the same, tragic way, but because of the evil of unrepentant sin, they would all experience the same tragedy and calamity of eternity in hell. Repentance and faith in Christ is the only way to escape the calamity of sin and eternal condemnation.

What is the greater calamity: God bringing judgment on an evil and undeserving world, or the evil that triggered His judgment in the first place? Is it the flood that engulfs the entire world or sin? Is it the fire and brimstone that rains down from heaven or sin? Is it the plagues which can destroy a nation or sin?

God can stop the flood, quench the fire, stay the plague, prevent the savage armies, deliver from affliction, and put an end to any other calamity or disaster with a simple word, or with a move from His mighty hand. But sin was a calamity that required God's only Son to address, reverse, and bring peace to. To drink up God's wrath was a serious thing. To taste death was a serious thing. To overcome death and destroy the works of the devil was a serious thing. The degree of God's response to the calamity shows the gravity of the calamity itself. There's no question about it — sin, death, and every moral evil that afflicts man is the greatest calamity, and there is no comparison.

That is why creation groans — not because of God's expressive judgment on sin (Psalm 96:11-13; Psalm 98:4-9), but because sin itself is a calamity; sin is the travesty on the tapestry of God's once-perfect universe (Romans 8:19-22). The calamities, disasters, and afflictions we experience are simply the outstretched branches linked to the main, tree trunk of the greatest calamity (evil and sin) which brought these other calamities to fruition.

While "calamity" does not fully capture the core meaning of evil in Isaiah 45:7, and it is not the argument I ascribe to, the term still points to the evil of sin and moral wickedness at its core. Even so, to accept this meaning is to overlook the unique distinction intended for this verse, and dismiss the consistent pattern and intent of creation language used in Isaiah 45:7.

CHAPTER 4 - GOD CREATED EVIL — A BIBLICAL ARGUMENT

Argument 3 — Evil is Simply the Absence of Good

The third popular argument is God did not create evil, for evil is the absence of good, and therefore, God cannot create something that has no essence or presence in the first place. This argument can be classified as the "privation theory of evil", and it is more of a philosophical argument than one pervading theological circles, but it is pervasive enough in Christianity that it should be properly addressed.

When this argument is put forth, apologists often use the analogy of darkness being the absence of light; darkness is dependent on the existence of light, and without it, darkness is void of its own actualized essence. Darkness is simply the empty byproduct of no light being present. Therefore, moral darkness ought to be perceived in the same way — evil is the absence of good (moral light), and has no actualized essence when good is not present, even though evil can be perceived and experienced. Apologists hereby conclude that like darkness, evil is simply the empty byproduct of no good being present.

Unfortunately, this is a flawed analogy and a flawed argument altogether. Because this is a philosophical argument, and not just a theological one, things can get convoluted very quickly, so I will use Scripture to be as succinct as possible. It can provide abundant clarity on positions that are thought to be somewhat murky. Scripture will rein us in from nebulous philosophy, and cut to the heart of the matter.

As far as the analogy goes, while there is some allure in it, we already debunked the presumption that darkness is the absence of light with the Bible; in Argument 1, we showed from Genesis 1 that God created darkness before the light, darkness was created as its own substance, and existed independently before God ever called the light into existence. God set up darkness to be divided from and contrasted to light, but biblically speaking, it is clearly not the absence of light. If darkness is an actual essence, and not light's missing presence, then the analogy championed among these apologists falls apart. If darkness is not the absence of light, the presupposition that evil is the absence of good should not be viable either.

With respect to the overall argument, evil cannot be the absence of good because as Isaiah 45:7 has stated, the Lord said He created evil. Creation is the result of God's positive acts; creation is God through His word and power bringing all things into existence. So when God creates, it is God actually doing something to cause what He intends to create to exist. It is a positive action with a positive result from the action. So when God says He creates evil, He is not creating the absence of something, which is essentially nothing, but He is creating the actual essence of something in and of itself. According to Isaiah 45:7, God creating evil was a positive act that resulted in a positive, actualized essence.

As an added note, it may not be intentional, but when we say evil is simply the absence of good, we unknowingly trivialize the importance of Christ's redemptive and atoning work on the cross. If evil is essentially nothing, on what grounds can God be angry against sin? For under this premise, God is mad about something that doesn't exist. On what grounds are we charged as sinners? For the nothingness of evil could not be quantified as the sin debt we owe to God. And on what grounds was Christ's death actually worth something? If evil holds no existential weight, what virtue could be gained from His sacrifice? Was Christ's death all a symbolic show with no effectual substance? God forbid!

The Son of God did not die for a non-quantity. Christ paid for *actual* sins that were forms of *actual* evil. To say evil is a non-existent entity is not just wrong, but it is highly offensive to Christ, who suffered the wrath of God to become the atonement for our sin and evil. It robs Christ of His glory.

CHAPTER 4 - GOD CREATED EVIL – A BIBLICAL ARGUMENT

Argument 4 – God is Not the Author of Sin and Evil

The final and hardest argument to address is that since God is holy, pure, true and good, then He can only create things that are holy, pure, true and good from the natural outflow of His character. Since God is a wholly good and all-benevolent Being, and is not evil, then it is impossible for God to create evil, for it is not a reflection of His character, and could not be the outflow of His inherent nature. If God were to create evil, then it means He is evil, which is not the case. Therefore, God cannot be the Author of sin and evil, so evil in the context of Isaiah 45:7 must mean something else. Apologists primarily rely on two Scripture passages to support this argument: 1 John 1:5 and James 1:13.

How can a good and holy God possibly create evil? This is the core, theological question for "theodicy", which is the argument that seeks to reconcile a good God with the problem of evil's existence in our world. While most are unfamiliar with the term, theodicy and its central question is still the most popular position many Christians take, but it is mainly based on unbiblical presumptions about the passages used to support their position. So to effectively tackle this argument, we have to address the unbiblical presumptions imposed on these verses, and dispel them with what the Bible actually says.

Starting with 1 John 1:5, the apologists make an unbiblical presumption about God's nature and attributes:

> This then is the message which we have heard of him, and declare unto you, that God is light, and in him is no darkness at all. - **1 John 1:5 (KJV)**

This verse speaks to God being light – not the natural, created light we are familiar with, but speaks to God being the emblem of moral light, which is the embodiment and epitome of moral goodness, holiness, purity and truth. The presence of light in God is contrasted to the absence of darkness in Him, for we learn that there is no darkness in God at all, which is the moral darkness that is attached to evil, sin, and moral wickedness. The LORD is not evil, sinful, or wicked in any wise (Job 34:10, 12).

All of what this Scripture aims to communicate is true. Where the presumption comes in is that since God is absolutely good, then it is absolutely impossible for Him to conceive or create evil. Based on the literal words of 1 John 1:5, why do we leap to such an erroneous conclusion? This verse speaks about God's attributes, not His ability. Nowhere in this passage does it explicitly say or imply that God could not create evil. It speaks about who God is, not about what He does. To conflate God being perfectly good to mean He cannot create evil is us trying to force the Bible to say what it doesn't say.

While God couldn't conceive of ever *doing* moral evil (James 1:13), to say that God could not even conceive of *creating* moral evil is a lie, for the triune God Himself told us He possessed the knowledge of good *and* evil; before evil and sin ever entered our world, the LORD had knowledge of evil as an eternal Being (Genesis 3:22). Whether it was defined by God at some point in eternity past, or this knowledge was always inherent to God's immutable and all-knowing Being, God already had the concept of evil within His mind. And since God is the Alpha and the Beginning of all things, the concept of evil had its beginning in God, which means it is possible for God to create what He conceives in His mind as the omnipotent Creator, as He did with every thing He created (Psalm 33:6; Revelation 4:11; John 1:3; Romans 11:36).

Hearing this, most Christians would then project their presumptions onto God and say if God created evil, then that means He *is* evil. Is God's *knowledge* of evil now the dark spot that stains His all-benevolent and morally good Being? By no means! Remember this: God can *be* what He says, and still *do* what He says without any of these things coming into conflict. If we hold to these presumptions about God and His relation to evil, we will inevitably compromise in believing God's Word.

Either we will keep our false assumptions about God in 1 John 1:5, and reject the statements about God's workings in Isaiah 45:7 (rejecting that He created evil), or we will keep our false assumptions about God in Isaiah 45:7, and reject the statements about God's nature in 1 John 1:5 (rejecting that God is good). In either case, we are saying God is a liar.

But if both Isaiah 45:7 *and* 1 John 1:5 are positively true statements about God — if God creates evil, which is a positive act that results in evil's actualized essence and expressions, yet God retains the quality of being purely good with no evil in His character, then it means that God can *create* evil without *being* evil (Psalm 145:17). Evil is in the hands of God, but it is not at the heart of God. We praise the LORD for that!

James 1:13 is the second pillar for presumption, as this Scripture is also used to strip God of His ability to create evil:

> Let no man say when he is tempted, I am tempted of God: for God cannot be tempted with evil, neither tempteth he any man: - **James 1:13 (KJV)**

The argument here is since the LORD cannot be tempted with evil, then He cannot create evil, for creating evil constitutes God being tempted with evil. While this is definitely the case with man, it is not the case with God. For man, being tempted with evil is a prerequisite to doing, engaging in, or creating evil from their sinful desires and imaginations (James 1:14-15; Romans 1:28-30; Genesis 3:6; 1 John 2:16-17; Matthew 6:13).

But for God, being tempted with evil is *not* a prerequisite for Him to create evil, especially knowing that God can create evil without being evil, which has been proven by affirming both Isaiah 45:7 and 1 John 1:5 as true. This presumption is the result of apologists playing fast and loose with the text. Take God at His literal word. What does God say about Himself in James 1:13? That He cannot be tempted with evil. That's it. Does God say He cannot create evil in this verse? No, and we shouldn't impose that meaning on something God *hasn't* said, primarily when that inference brings James 1:13 into theological conflict with Isaiah 45:7. Again, if we stand on unbiblical presumptions, we will eventually put ourselves in a theological dilemma, and will compromise God's Word to solve the dilemma.

> Faith which accepts one word of God and rejects another is not faith in God, but faith in our own judgment or our own taste. - **Charles H. Spurgeon**

We don't need to compromise on God's Word, for all of Scripture is true altogether (Psalm 19:9). With Isaiah 45:7 being true, what does James 1:13 mean? God is not tempted by evil's essence; He is not allured by the essence He created, nor is He tempted to indulge in the forms and expressions of evil's essence, for they run contrary to His morally good and unchangeable nature. God can create moral evil without being tempted to do moral evil. This brings Isaiah 45:7 and James 1:13 in alignment with each other.

There are other Scriptures that can be used to support theodicy — Deuteronomy 32:4, Psalm 92:15, Habakkuk 1:13 and 1 Corinthians 14:33 — but apologists will apply the same faulty presumptions to deny the truth of Isaiah 45:7, seeking to absolve the LORD for creating evil. But let God be true, and every man a liar (Romans 3:4). Every verse supporting theodicy affirms who God is, but when apologists lead with their unbiblical presumptions, they will sacrifice Isaiah 45:7 for their argument, and place constraints on God that He didn't call for, which sadly makes them liars for not embracing the *whole* counsel of God, however inconvenient it may be. God created evil, and no theological argument will ever change this truth.

When it comes to theodicy, the way its supporting Scriptures are used follow a pattern — apologists tend infer on what God has *not* said as the basis for their arguments, while what God *has* said about creating evil is rejected or construed to mean something else. To keep ourselves from error, we should all apply Charles Spurgeon's words of wisdom when interpreting the Bible:

When Scripture is silent, you be silent. - **Charles H. Spurgeon**

ABSOLVING GOD FOR EVIL DOES GOD NO GOOD

As we inspected each of these arguments, I have been on the defensive to protect what Isaiah 45:7 has to say, but now it's time to go on the offensive. For Christians who believe God is not the Author of evil and sin, if I ask you where evil came from, what would your answer be? I suspect most Christians would likely give me one of three answers. Option 1, evil came from Satan and man's sin; Option 2, evil came from out of nowhere; or Option 3, we do not know where evil came from.

If you don't know where evil came from, that's okay — that is why this book was written, so it's okay if you ascribe to Option 3 for now, as you are reading this book to discover the biblical answer. However, those who ascribe to Option 1 or 2 can be refuted, for there are biblical arguments to show why these schools of thought are wrong.

We will close out the chapter examining these answers, not only to show why they are incorrect, but show how holding to these positions does God a great disservice.

Option 1 – Evil Came from Satan and Man's Sin

Instead of God being the Author of evil and sin, many Christians believe that evil and sin first originated with Satan, and evil and sin was later introduced into humanity and creation through Adam's disobedience. Satan and Adam are marked as the source of evil's existence. While some parts of this viewpoint are true, other aspects of this idea contain falsehoods which can be remedied with a closer look at Scripture.

Why do Christians believe that evil and sin originated with Satan? Because based on Jesus' words in John 8:44, many presume that to be the case. Let's see this from Scripture. After the murderous Pharisees boasted of their relation to Abraham, they began claiming God was their father, but Jesus enlightened them on who their true father was:

> Ye are of *your* father the devil, and the lusts of your father ye will do. He was a murderer from the beginning, and abode not in the truth, because there is no truth in him. When he speaketh a lie, he speaketh of his own: for he is a liar, and the father of it. - **John 8:44 (KJV)**

Though they were physical descendants of Abraham, Jesus let the Pharisees and Jews know they were the spiritual children of Satan. Their conduct and rejection of the truth was the tangible proof of that spiritual reality. Sin joins all men to Satan's family tree, and Christ lets the Pharisees (and us) know that their sinful desires descended from their spiritual father, the devil, for Satan was the spiritual ancestor of manifest sin and evil.

In other words, Satan was the very first sinner within God's creation, even before Adam and Eve. The Bible doesn't tell us exactly when Satan sinned against God, but we can biblically deduce that Satan's fall occurred between the end of Genesis 2 and the beginning of Genesis 3. I say this for a few reasons (this is a quick tangent, but please bear with me).

One, even with evil's essence being created, God classified His entire creation as very good (Genesis 1:31), or working in perfect harmony, for evil was not present or manifest anywhere in creation at that point. Two, within the six-day creation, the LORD created Satan — or Lucifer as he was once known — to be a perfect being like all of His creatures (Ezekiel 28:12, 14; Nehemiah 9:6; Psalm 33:6; Psalm 146:5-6; Psalm 103:19-21; Job 38:4-7; Exodus 20:11).

Three, God makes it known that Lucifer has been to the garden of Eden (Ezekiel 28:13), which not only alludes to his presence in Eden as Satan, but directly reinforces that Lucifer was allowed into Eden as a perfect being prior to his fall. God planted the garden of Eden in Genesis 2 (Genesis 2:8), Satan made his evil presence known in Genesis 3; therefore, Lucifer was a perfect being at the time of Genesis 2, but sinned and became Satan prior to the events of Genesis 3, which puts his fall between these points in time, making him the spiritual father or ancestor of sin and evil manifested in creation. That title belongs to Satan, not Adam and Eve, for he was recorded as the first creature to ever sin against God (Genesis 3:6).

But does being the spiritual ancestor of sin and evil equate to Satan being the *author* of evil's existence? No, not at all. Satan became the spiritual ancestor for sin and evil because of a free choice he made, not because he authored evil into existence. Evil existed prior to Satan's fall, which means Satan was *not* the creative source of evil. To prove this, we need to analyze how Lucifer fell in the first place.

Observe Ezekiel 28, one of the two principal passages that speaks to Lucifer's fall:

> Moreover the word of the LORD came unto me, saying, Son of man, take up a lamentation upon the king of Tyrus, and say unto him, Thus saith the Lord GOD; <u>Thou sealest up the sum, full of wisdom, and perfect in beauty.</u> Thou hast been in Eden the garden of God; every precious stone *was* thy covering, the sardius, topaz, and the diamond, the beryl, the onyx, and the jasper, the sapphire, the emerald, and the carbuncle, and gold: the workmanship of thy tabrets and of thy pipes was prepared in thee in the day that thou wast created. <u>Thou *art* the anointed cherub that covereth; and I have set thee *so*:</u> thou wast upon the holy mountain of God; thou hast walked up and down in the midst of the stones of fire. <u>Thou *wast* perfect in thy ways from the day that thou wast created, till iniquity was found in thee. By the multitude of thy merchandise they have filled the midst of thee with violence, and thou hast sinned:</u> therefore I will cast thee as profane out of the mountain of God: and I will destroy thee, O covering cherub, from the midst of the stones of fire. - **Ezekiel 28:11-16 (KJV)**

Take note of verse 15. "Thou *wast* perfect in thy ways from the day that thou wast created, till iniquity was found in thee." From the very beginning, God created Lucifer as a perfect being with a peculiar glory, but there was one day where the LORD discovered sin at work within his once-good and perfect creature. In a nutshell, Lucifer's sin was the sin of pride. As the anointed cherub, Lucifer was a perfect and privileged being, but he began to see how wise and beautiful he was — how bright he shined in God's kingdom (Ezekiel 28:16). Lucifer no longer wanted to serve God, but set his sights on higher things:

> <u>How art thou fallen from heaven, O Lucifer, son of the morning!</u> *how* art thou cut down to the ground, which didst

weaken the nations! <u>For thou hast said in thine heart, I will ascend into heaven, I will exalt my throne above the stars of God: I will sit also upon the mount of the congregation, in the sides of the north: I will ascend above the heights of the clouds; I will be like the most High.</u> Yet thou shalt be brought down to hell, to the sides of the pit. - **Isaiah 14:12-15 (KJV)**

In his pride, Lucifer wanted to equate himself with God. He wanted to exalt himself in heaven and be worshipped. Lucifer rejected God's designated place for him, and he sought to be the master of his own fate. But the anointed cherub only sealed his eternal fate, for "pride *goeth* before destruction, and an haughty spirit before a fall" (Proverbs 16:18). For this rebellious desire, Lucifer became spiritually defiled, the LORD stripped him of his privilege and position, and he lost his place in heaven.

Satan's fall teaches us something about God's creatures, and why Satan nor any other creature is the source of evil's existence except God alone. When God created His creatures, He endowed them with certain qualities, features and capabilities. He gave the eagle its wings to fly, and the leopard its spots; He gave the spider the ability to produce silk and weave webs, designed the bee to make honey, and allowed the fish to breathe underwater and maneuver through the sea. You get the idea.

However, these endowments are not limited to external factors, but the LORD also endowed His creatures with internal qualities and capabilities. Take man as an example:

<u>And God said, Let us make man in our image, after our likeness:</u> and let them have dominion over the fish of the sea, and over the fowl of the air, and over the cattle, and

and over all the earth, and over every creeping thing that creepeth upon the earth. <u>So God created man in his *own* image, in the image of God created he him; male and female created he them.</u> - **Genesis 1:26–27 (KJV)**

We know man was created in God's image and likeness, but this image and likeness does not pertain to God's external or visible attributes, for God is a Spirit, and does not have a physical form (John 4:24; Luke 24:36-40). Man was not created to be the reflection of God's *physical* form. To be made in God's image and likeness was for mankind to inherit and reflect God's spiritual nature, capacities and characteristics — the qualities that are internal or inherent to God. The LORD later gave man a physical form for His image and likeness to be housed in, primarily for man to interact with the physical world, and exercise those internal capabilities through a physical vessel (Genesis 2:7, 21-23).

The LORD endowed man with internal qualities and capacities that gave us the ability to do various things. Without these endowments being bestowed, man could never do what God never gave him the ability to do. Whether they be external or internal, all of our abilities, capabilities, and capacities come from God, for in Him "we live, and move, and have our being" (Acts 17:28).

It seems Satan and the angels were made in a similar way; they were not made in the image of God as man was, but were also given the same capability that man was, which is a *freed will*. A freed will is the God-given ability to choose within the conceivable parameters of God-defined choices; a freed will is what allows a creature to rationally and wilfully choose between good and evil. We see this exercise of a freed will among the angels in Lucifer's fall, and we see this among the fallen angels — known as the sons of God — in Noah's time, who left their heavenly estate to copulate with the daughters of men, which led to giant offspring (the Nephilim) on the earth (Genesis 6:1-4; Jude 1:6; 2 Peter 2:4). Angels can choose between good and evil because of the freed will God gave them. Therefore, when angels choose evil, it is because God gave them the capacity to wilfully choose it.

So when iniquity was found in Lucifer, it was simply the sinful expression of a capacity that was embedded in Lucifer to begin with, which was using his will to choose between good and evil. If evil never existed, Satan could never choose it, for it would not have been built into the capacities and capabilities of his available choices. If good was his only conceptual choice, then Lucifer would always be good, and Satan could never come into being, for his nature would be constrained to the capacity of only being good.

Through his sinful choice, Satan became a manifest *expression* of evil's pre-existing essence, but not the *source* of evil itself. Through his sinful choice, Satan's exposure to evil's essence corrupted his entire nature; he lost every good attribute, and forever inherited the nature of a liar and a murderer (John 8:44).

In this case, man is no different from Satan, and should be absolved of the accusation for being the creative source of evil. If Satan is the first sinner in creation, and the spiritual ancestor of manifest sin and evil, but is not the source of evil, then all of his spiritual children and descendants cannot be the source of evil's creation and existence, which absolves mankind from this audacious claim.

Like Satan and the angels, God also gave man a freed will to choose between the outlined parameters of good and evil (Genesis 2:15-17; Deuteronomy 30:15-20). While man did not possess the *knowledge* of good and evil until the fall (Genesis 3:6), they were made with the *capacity* to choose good or evil from the very beginning. Adam and Eve were made with an inclination toward good, but with a capacity in their freed will to choose evil. Before the fall, all man possessed was the knowledge of good, for they were enraptured within all the elements that God called good. Adam and Eve were given a freed will, where they could choose between good or evil according to God, and they would be fully responsible for their choice. Good and evil were set before them, and they chose to do evil.

When man fell, man lost the privileges of a freed will, and came under the power and bondage of sin, where we are depraved and are inclined to evil. Through Adam's sinful choice, his exposure to evil's essence corrupted his entire nature and race; humanity lost every good attribute, became spiritually dead, and like our spiritual ancestor Satan, we all inherited the evil nature as creatures now enslaved to the power of sin (Genesis 6:5; Genesis 8:21; Isaiah 59:1-16; Jeremiah 17:9; Matthew 15:18-20; Matthew 19:17; Mark 7:20-23; Mark 10:18; Luke 18:19; John 3:16-21; John 8:34; Romans 3:11-18; Romans 6:16-17; Romans 7:14-25; Ephesians 2:1-3). Like Satan, through Adam's sinful choice, humanity became a manifest *expression* of evil's pre-existing essence, but not the *source* of evil itself.

This is further reinforced by Romans 5:12, which gives insight into evil's manifest effect on the world through Adam's sin:

> Wherefore, as by one man sin entered into the world, and death by sin; and so death passed upon all men, for that all have sinned: - **Romans 5:12 (KJV)**

Words matter, and we live by God's every word in Scripture (Matthew 4:4). Here the Bible tells us sin and death *entered* into the world, which means sin and death were already prepared in the event of Adam's disobedience (Genesis 2:17); sin and death — forms of evil — were not spontaneously created by man outside of God once Adam disobeyed; sin and death were already being kept in reserve, and were being held back like waters in a dam. Adam's disobedience broke the levee, which allowed these evils that God prepared as punishment to flow into our world. Man was never the creative source of evil.

The LORD created evil, but man perpetuated evil. Man is the reason evil is manifest our world. God was sovereign over evil's creation, and sovereign over the circumstances for evil being unleashed in the world, but man is responsible for actually unleashing evil into creation. Through Adam, man took hold of evil by sinning against God. God was sovereign. Man was responsible.

Satan and Adam are the catalysts of evil's *presence* in the world, but are not the cause of evil's *existence* in creation — that can only be ascribed to God alone. Satan and Adam took their embedded capacity to choose between good and evil, and used their will to choose evil. This led to evil being expressed in the world; it did not lead to the creation of evil itself.

While God wants the credit for evil's creation, He cannot be credited for evil's proliferation — God is not responsible for propagating evil; God did not unleash evil on our world, Satan and Adam did that. In accordance with God's sovereignty, it was predestined that evil would be unleashed for God's purposes, but God did not do the unleashing of evil. Satan and Adam are not the source of evil's essence and existence, so Option 1 as an answer cannot be true. Crediting evil to Satan or Adam robs God of the glory for His creation.

Before I move on, I just want to magnify the LORD. Look at how marvelous God is — Satan acquaints himself with evil, and he is utterly corrupted by it; Adam acquaints with himself with evil, and he and all mankind are utterly corrupted by it. But God is even more acquainted with evil as its Creator, and has a deeper and fuller understanding of evil as the omniscient God (John 2:24-25), yet God has never been tempted by evil, nor has the knowledge or existence of evil ever corrupted His holy and good nature. Moral evil has stained Satan and humanity black, but God's intimate knowledge and acquaintance with evil has never changed His shade. God is unlike any other Being, and this should leave us in awe of Him.

Option 2 – Evil Came from Out of Nowhere

As an alternative view, rather than God, Satan or Adam being the authors for evil and sin, evil has no author and has always existed as an entity. Evil is not a created essence, but exists without an origin. Essentially, evil's origin is a mystery with no biblical explanation available. This option is not as popular as Option 1, but it is a viewpoint which exists among Christians, theologians, and philosophers. However, this viewpoint not only comes into conflict with Scripture, but comes into conflict with God Himself.

First of all, evil existing without an origin is false, for Isaiah 45:7 has already established that evil's origin is with God, so here is where this premise is explicitly defeated by Scripture. Secondly, what brings this viewpoint into conflict with God can be explained in Exodus 3, where the LORD offers one of the greatest revelations to Moses at the burning bush:

> And God said unto Moses, I AM THAT I AM: and he said, Thus shalt thou say unto the children of Israel, I AM hath sent me unto you. - **Exodus 3:14 (KJV)**

As I've mentioned earlier in the chapter, God being the "I AM THAT I AM" (IATIA) speaks to His aseity, the characteristic of

CHAPTER 4 - GOD CREATED EVIL – A BIBLICAL ARGUMENT

God being both self-existent and self-sufficient as a Being. Self-existence is the idea that God exists all on His own; God has always existed as a Being, and has never relied on any other person or thing *to* exist. While He depends on nothing to exist, all things depend on Him to exist. There was no one or nothing before the LORD (Genesis 1:1; Isaiah 43:10-11; Isaiah 44:6-8; Isaiah 45:5-6, 18; John 1:1-3; Exodus 3:14; John 8:58).

Self-sufficiency represents God's ability to eternally sustain His own existence, without depending on anyone or anything outside of Himself. God is sufficient to sustain God, and His existence is not exhausted or threatened, for God's sustaining power is perpetual and eternal (Acts 17:24-25; Isaiah 40:28; Psalm 121:4; Psalm 50:12). Self-existence and self-sufficiency are tied together to communicate God's aseity.

God being the IATIA destroys the possibility of Option 2, and here's why: when God says He is the I AM THAT I AM, He is not only saying that there is no *one* like Him; He did not say "I AM *WHO* I AM" to differentiate Himself from persons and individuals, but said "I AM *THAT* I AM" to differentiate Himself from persons and things. There is no one or no *thing* like Him; nobody or nothing is self-existent like God is. Nobody or nothing is self-sufficient like God is. No one or nothing can claim aseity, for only God possesses it, and that is why He alone can truthfully say that He is the "I AM THAT I AM".

Since God cannot lie (Titus 1:2; Hebrews 6:18), when He says "I AM THAT I AM", it is a truthful representation of who He alone is, for "I" is singular, which means that no one or nothing else can be the subject of this pronoun except Himself. If the LORD alone is self-existent and self-sufficient, nothing else can be, and therefore, all things exist through Him (John 1:3) and all things are sustained by Him, including sin and evil (Colossians 1:16-17; Romans 11:36).

If evil is actually some*thing*, then this *thing* was created, for all created things proceed from God. If evil was never created, then evil would be nothing, for it could never exist apart from all the things God created. Evil did not spawn out of nowhere; evil does not have life within itself to do this — to exist on its own. Only God has life within Himself (John 5:26; John 1:1-4; Romans 8:10-11; 1 John 5:11-12).

If you say that God did not create evil, but you also say that evil came out of nowhere, then evil is also self-existent (existing outside of God's creative power) and self-sufficient (consisting outside of God's sustaining power). If evil is both self-existent and self-sufficient, then God is a liar, for He can no longer be or ever was the "I AM THAT I AM".

If evil is both self-existent and self-sufficient, then the "I" in the IATIA statement is false, and God cannot make that claim, for there is something that self-exists and self-sustains alongside Him, which is evil. If evil is like God in these things, then God must reframe His IATIA statement by saying "WE ARE THAT WE ARE" to include evil, or evil itself can boast and say "I AM THAT I AM ALSO!" to equate itself with God. Either way, these are the spiritual gymnastics we have to perform to give evil its aseity. In any case, it leads us malign and blaspheme the God who cannot lie.

God said there is no God before Him, beside Him, and after Him (Isaiah 43:10-11; Isaiah 44:6-8; Isaiah 45:5-6; Deuteronomy 32:39), and there is no God greater than Him, for He is the highest Being of all (Hebrews 6:13; Psalm 97:9). There is none greater or equal to God in any facet or measure, and that includes evil. Evil cannot claim self-sufficiency. Evil cannot claim self-existence. Those attributes belong to God alone. And if evil cannot claim self-existence or self-sufficiency, it must exist because it was created, and must persist because it is being sustained by Something other than itself.

CHAPTER 4 - GOD CREATED EVIL – A BIBLICAL ARGUMENT

> Nothing that God has made is self-existent. Self-existence belongs exclusively to the "I AM THAT I AM." - **Charles H. Spurgeon**

Evil gets it provenance from God. Provenance is the beginning of something's origin and existence, or a record of ownership for a work or object, which is used to affirm the authenticity of something. The biblical fallacies associated with Options 1 and 2 leave us with no other conclusion: God is the creative source behind evil itself.

> And that there is no power, either of light or darkness, of good or evil, of happiness or misery, independent of the One Supreme God, infinite in power and in goodness. - **Robert Lowth**

Other Considerations for God Being Evil's Creator

Way back in Chapter 2, I mentioned that the LORD is sovereign over evil, and every form of evil. Satan, sin, death, the flesh, the world, demons, wicked men and hell — whether it involves their creation, their functionality, their sustenance or their destruction, the LORD is sovereign over evil in every regard. Every form of evil serves God's purposes in some way or another.

The LORD created these forms of evil, and sustains these forms of evil (Isaiah 45:7; Colossians 1:16-17; Romans 11:36; John 1:1-3). God is supreme over these forms of evil, and each form of evil is God's servant (Proverbs 16:4; Exodus 7:8-13; Job 1:6-12; Job 2:1-7; 1 Samuel 16:14-23; 1 Kings 22:13-23; Luke 4:31-37; Acts 10:38; John 11:40-44; 1 Corinthians 15:50-57; John 10:14-18; John 6:33; 1 John 4:4; Romans 9:17; Hebrews 12:9; 1 John 3:8). God can restrain these forms of evil (Psalm 76:10; Genesis 11:1-9; Genesis 20:1-7; Matthew 16:18; 2

Thessalonians 2:1-12). And He is so sovereign over evil, He can even bring good out of evil (Genesis 45:4-8; Genesis 50:15-21; Esther 7:7-10; Isaiah 53; Acts 2:22-24; Acts 3:11-26; Acts 4:26-28; Romans 8:28, 35-39). After these forms of evil have served their purpose, the LORD will abolish and destroy each form of evil forevermore (2 Peter 3:10-13; 1 John 2:16-17; 1 Corinthians 15:22-26; Revelation 19:11-21; Revelation 20:7-15; Revelation 21:1-8, 27).

Consider all the ways God exercises His sovereignty and power over evil. Based on what the Bible presents, is it logical to think that God can be the Controller and Consummator of evil, but not the creative Cause behind evil itself? When it comes to evil, God can only be the Omega, but He can't be the Alpha? That is inconsistent with Scripture. The LORD can bring an end to evil because He created it, and has sustained its existence from the very beginning.

GOD CREATES EVIL

To finalize my biblical argument, I'm going to show you examples of God creating moral evil in real-time within the biblical narrative. We can see God creating moral evil when He defines it in His Word. God creates evil when He defines it.

I want you to visualize evil's created essence like a lump of clay; like the potter at the wheel, who adds clay to the lump to reshape its form, or removes clay from the lump to refine its form, God can manipulate evil's essence in the same way — as the Potter of creation, He can add to evil's defined essence, and increase the scope of moral evil and sin, and in the same vein, God can also remove from evil's defined essence, and decrease the scope of moral evil and sin through His Word (Romans 5:13; Romans 7:7-13).

Sin (moral evil) is the transgression of the law (1 John 3:4). The "law" is either God's word implicitly written upon man's heart and conscience (Romans 2:12-15), or the explicit revelation of God's word through written Scripture (Exodus 31:18; Deuteronomy 30:10; Joshua 1:8; 2 Kings 22:8-13; Psalm 19:7-11; Psalm 119; John 20:30-31; 2 Timothy 3:16-17; 2 Peter 1:19-21). To transgress the law in either sense is to commit sin. However, sin cannot be imputed where there is no law present (Romans 5:13).

As God creates moral evil in the biblical narrative, we can see the law which defines sin being amended and repealed by God, and therefore, sin and moral evil being redefined as a result. Though mankind embodies and expresses evil, evil was never shaped by man, but evil was shaped by the LORD who defines what evil is. Let's explore how God creates evil with four, biblical examples.

Incest

Incest is the sin of marrying or having sex with a close or traceable relative. God marked the practice of incest as a sin during the Israelites' sojourn through the wilderness (Leviticus 18:1-18; Leviticus 20:11-23). Prior to these commands, there were incestuous relationships which existed that were lawful, and were not counted as sin, for the law against this practice was not given to men up until this point.

Lawful, incestuous relationships include Adam and Eve, Abraham and Sarah, and Moses' parents, Amram and Jochebed. Adam and Eve were husband and wife, even though they were physically related, for Eve was formed out of Adam's taken rib (Genesis 2:21-24). At this point in time and era in history, relatives marrying and having children together was acceptable, for it is how the earth became populated, and it was in fulfillment of the mandate to be fruitful and multiply (Genesis 1:28; Genesis 4:17).

Abraham married Sarah, who was his half-sister through

Abraham's father (Genesis 20:18). And Moses' father, Amram married his aunt, Jochebed, who later became the mother of Aaron and Moses (Exodus 6:20). Because there was no law against it, none of these aforementioned relationships were guilty of incest.

But once God defined incest as sin, what was once an acceptable practice became evil because it now violates the law of the One who spoke it as such, and commanded us not to do it. After this point, every instance of an incestuous relationship was counted as sin, and condemned as an evil thing (2 Samuel 13:1-21; 1 Corinthians 5). Through His commands, the scope of evil was expanded to include incest. God redefined evil to include incest. Incest was lumped into evil's created essence.

Murder

According to Scripture, murder is the intentional, premeditated, and unlawful killing of another person. It does not just consist of the "act" of killing, but is linked with the "intent" to kill. Murder was unlawful since Cain's time, for the LORD warned Cain that if he gave in to his anger, he would sin; that sin resulted in the murder of Abel (Genesis 4:1-8; 1 John 3:12; Matthew 15:19; Mark 7:21). Cain's murder violated the law upon his heart, and the command issued by God.

After the flood, God implemented the death penalty for murder by civil government, as God saw it as the appropriate punishment for this crime committed against one of God's image-bearers (Genesis 9:6; Exodus 20:13; Leviticus 24:17-22). This law of life has never changed for humanity since then, and the death penalty was not to be executed by the individual, but was entrusted to the civil government after due process was exercised for the accused (Romans 13:1-4; Numbers 35:30; Deuteronomy 17:6; Deuteronomy 19:15-21; Hebrews 10:28; Proverbs 20:22; Romans 12:19; Hebrews 10:30; Psalm 94:1).

CHAPTER 4 - GOD CREATED EVIL – A BIBLICAL ARGUMENT

The death penalty was reserved for those who *physically* murdered someone; this punishment was God's just response for the *sin* and *crime* of murder (1 Timothy 1:8-11; Romans 7:12). To give someone the death penalty without due process, or to withhold this penalty after being rightfully convicted was sin, and a miscarriage of justice (Ecclesiates 8:11; Deuteronomy 19:11-13; Numbers 35:31-34; Proverbs 24:11-12; Proverbs 28:17; Exodus 21:14; 1 Kings 21:1-16; Matthew 26:59-61; Matthew 27:15-26; John 8:1-11; Deuteronomy 16:18-20; Exodus 23:1-8; Proverbs 17:23; Exodus 20:16; Proverbs 18:17). Here we see the evil of murder is well-defined by God.

However, when we get to Jesus' time, the Son of God amends the existing law, and expands on what constitutes murder during His ministry:

> Ye have heard that it was said by them of old time, Thou shalt not kill; and whosoever shall kill shall be in danger of the judgment: <u>But I say unto you, That whosoever is angry with his brother without a cause shall be in danger of the judgment: and whosoever shall say to his brother, Raca, shall be in danger of the council: but whosoever shall say, Thou fool, shall be in danger of hell fire.</u> - **Matthew 5:21-22 (KJV)**

Because of Christ's amendment, unjustified anger towards someone, along with vicious language used to slander, demean, and dehumanize a fellow image-bearer now became equal to the *sin* of murder, for these are the conditions in the heart and on the tongue which lead to the *crime* of murder. While civil government can prosecute man for the crime of physical murder, only God can convict and condemn a man for the spiritual murder that manifests in his heart, and flows out from his lips. Prior to the amendment, only physical murder was counted as sin, but once the amendment was made, what constituted murder was redefined and expanded. God created moral evil by expanding the scope of murder as a sin.

Adultery

For a majority of the Bible, adultery consisted of a man or woman physically having sex with a married person that is not their spouse, which thereby violates the sanctity of the marriage covenant between spouses. God condemned adultery in the law of Moses, and it was a capital offence (Exodus 20:14; Leviticus 20:10; Deuteronomy 5:18; Deuteronomy 22:22). Up until Christ, adultery was defined as evil within this purview.

However, as He did with murder, God creates moral evil as Christ amends the law, and enlarges the scope for the sin of adultery on two, different occasions:

> Ye have heard that it was said by them of old time, Thou shalt not commit adultery: <u>But I say unto you, That whosoever looketh on a woman to lust after her hath committed adultery with her already in his heart.</u> - **Matthew 5:27-28 (KJV)**

> <u>And I say unto you, Whosoever shall put away his wife, except *it be* for fornication, and shall marry another, committeth adultery: and whoso marrieth her which is put away doth commit adultery.</u> - **Matthew 19:9 (KJV)**

In the first instance, adultery was no longer limited to the physical act with a *married* person, but now extended to *any* woman or man being objectified through the lust in a person's heart. As the Lawgiver, Jesus causes adultery to involve the spiritual act in the heart, not just the physical act in the body. In the second passage, the parameters for adultery are further expanded to involve the unlawful grounds for remarriage. Unless the divorce is based on prior, undisclosed fornication, there are no lawful grounds for remarriage. If a man divorces his wife for any other reason outside of prior, undisclosed fornication, he commits adultery if he marries another woman, and the divorced woman commits adultery if she is married to another man.

There are only two ways for unlawfully divorced spouses to be remarried: one of the divorced spouses has to die to annul the existing marriage (Romans 7:2-3), or the divorced spouses must be reconciled to each other (1 Corinthians 7:10-11). Remarriage outside of these conditions constitutes adultery. With each instance, the LORD adds to evil's essence by creating additional criteria for the sin of adultery. Moral evil is created at His word.

Eating Unclean Meats
With this topic, we are going see the LORD both increasing and constricting the scope of moral evil at different points in the biblical narrative; as we progress through Scripture, you will see figurative lumps of clay being added or removed from evil's defined essence through God's law being amended and repealed.

When man was created, God restricted man and the animals to a herbivore diet, which consisted of herbs from seed-bearing plants and fruits from seed-bearing trees (Genesis 1:29-30). This was the lawful diet mandated for mankind at creation. Any deviation from this diet would be unlawful, and would thereby be considered sin.

After the flood, the LORD begins to expand man's diet, and now gives man the permission to eat any creature on earth; only the blood of a creature could not be eaten (Genesis 9:2-4). What was once unlawful became lawful at God's word, and the new scope of man's diet comes with new prohibitions attached. The scope of an unlawful diet took on a new shape.

Before reaching Canaan, the Israelites were given dietary laws that separated clean meats (Leviticus 11:1-12), which were permissible to eat, from unclean meats which were now forbidden from being eaten (Leviticus 11:13-47). In this epoch of biblical history, God creates evil by once again constricting the sphere of man's lawful diet, as creatures marked as unclean were excluded from the diet. Going forward, any partakers who ate these unclean foods were committing sin and abominations before the LORD. This amendment to man's diet again redefined what constituted moral evil.

Once we reach the church age, after Christ died, rose and ascended, the Holy Spirit makes it known through the Apostle Paul that God has made a final amendment on man's, lawful diet, and the restrictions ratified in the law of Moses are now abolished:

> <u>Now the Spirit speaketh expressly,</u> that in the latter times some shall depart from the faith, giving heed to seducing spirits, and doctrines of devils; Speaking lies in hypocrisy; having their conscience seared with a hot iron; Forbidding to marry, <u>*and commanding* to abstain from meats, which God hath created to be received with thanksgiving of them which believe and know the truth. For every creature of God *is* good, and nothing to be refused, if it be received with thanksgiving: For it is sanctified by the word of God and prayer.</u> - **1 Timothy 4:1-5 (KJV)**

This final amendment to man's diet was foreshadowed with Apostle Peter's encounter with Cornelius (Acts 10:9-48; Acts 11:1-18), and foreshadowed with the council at Jerusalem regarding the Christian Gentiles (Acts 15:1-31), but in the passage above, this final amendment to man's diet is explicitly codified. The restrictions in the law of Moses have been repealed, but the dietary laws given to Noah post-flood still apply (Genesis 9:2-4), yet in the church age we are in, no creature is viewed as unclean and are once again permissible to eat. The amendment through God's word sanctifies all creatures, and makes them lawful to eat once it is received by prayer. This final iteration of man's diet is God's final delineation between good and evil, and involves the constraints of the diet being relaxed for all men.

These four examples clearly show God creating evil through the biblical narrative; God creates evil when He defines it. He shapes and reshapes evil's defined essence by His word. By His word, what was once considered acceptable could later be defined as evil, and what was once considered evil could later be defined as acceptable (Isaiah 5:20-21). Thankfully, there are no more amendments and repealments for evil and sin, for the canon of Scripture is now closed (2 Timothy 3:16-17; 2 Peter 1:2-4; Deuteronomy 4:2; Deuteronomy 12:32; Psalm 12:6-7; Proverbs 30:5-6; Revelation 22:18-19; Psalm 119:89). Evil is what evil will be until the end of time, but it has always been the LORD who has defined it. God creates evil (Isaiah 45:7).

CONCLUSION

The creation of evil is not a mystery; it may not be prominently discussed since many don't properly understand it, but it is not a mystery. There are mysteries in the Bible which God has stated to be mysteries, yet there are things which God has explicitly laid out that we make into mysteries ourselves due to our lack of understanding (Psalm 119:34, 73, 99, 104, 125, 130). Isaiah 45:7 demystifies the mystery of evil, and gives us the green light to search the Scriptures and search out the matter for a biblical answer (Proverbs 25:2; John 5:39).

Therefore hearken unto me, ye men of understanding: far be it from God, *that he should do* wickedness; and *from* the Almighty, *that he should commit* iniquity.

JOB 34:10 (KJV)

Good Thou art, and good Thou dost,
Thy mercies reach to all,
Chiefly those who on Thee trust,
And for Thy mercy call;
New they every morning are;
As fathers when their children cry,
Us Thou dost in pity spare,
And all our wants supply.

Mercy o'er Thy works presides;
Thy providence displayed
Still preserves, and still provides
For all Thy hands have made;
Keeps, with most distinguished care,
The man who on Thy love depends;
Watches every numbered hair,
And all his steps attends.

Who can sound the depths unknown
Of Thy redeeming grace?
Grace that gave Thine only Son
To save a ruined race!
Millions of transgressors poor
Thou hast for Jesus' sake forgiven,
Made them of Thy favor sure,
And snatched from hell to Heaven.

Millions more Thou ready art
To save, and to forgive;
Every soul and every heart
Of man Thou wouldst receive:
Father, now accept of mine,
Which now, through Christ, I offer Thee;
Tell me now, in love divine,
That Thou hast pardoned me!

Charles Wesley

CHAPTER 5
Is God Evil? Is God An Evildoer?

Therefore hearken unto me, ye men of understanding: far be it from God, *that he should do* wickedness; and *from* the Almighty, *that he should commit* iniquity.
Job 34:10 (KJV)

I could end this book with the previous chapter, but the answers provided in Chapter 4 carry their own implications, and opens the door for more questions. I want this book to be a comprehensive exploration of evil, so I will spend the rest of book trying to answer these questions using the Bible.

If we accept the fact that God created evil, we might begin to reason that God Himself is evil, or presume that He is an evildoer for creating evil. However, none of these assumptions are true, and hopefully, I've clearly dispelled those assumptions with Scripture in Chapter 4. To avoid becoming redundant, this will be a relatively short chapter, but I hope it will provide more clarity regarding God's relationship to evil.

IS GOD EVIL?

No, God is not evil. As I stated in Chapter 4, God creating evil does not *make* Him evil — God can create evil without *being* evil, for evil is in the creative hands of God, but it is not at the heart of God (Psalm 145:17; Psalm 5:4; Psalm 92:15). The God of the Bible is purely good, and we know that to be the case for the Bible tells us so:

And the LORD passed by before him, and proclaimed, The LORD, The LORD God, merciful and gracious, longsuffering, and abundant in goodness and truth, - **Exodus 34:6 (KJV)**

Good and upright *is* the LORD: therefore will he teach sinners in the way. - **Psalm 25:8 (KJV)**

O taste and see that the LORD *is* good: blessed *is* the man *that* trusteth in him. - **Psalm 34:8 (KJV)**

For thou, Lord, *art* good, and ready to forgive; and plenteous in mercy unto all them that call upon thee. - **Psalm 86:5 (KJV)**

For the LORD *is* good; his mercy *is* everlasting; and his truth *endureth* to all generations. - **Psalm 100:5 (KJV)**

Oh that *men* would praise the LORD *for* his goodness, and *for* his wonderful works to the children of men! - **Psalm 107:8 (KJV)**

Thou *art* good, and doest good; teach me thy statutes. - **Psalm 119:68 (KJV)**

Teach me to do thy will; for thou *art* my God: thy spirit *is* good; lead me into the land of uprightness. - **Psalm 143:10 (KJV)**

The LORD *is* good to all: and his tender mercies *are* over all his works. - **Psalm 145:9 (KJV)**

The LORD *is* righteous in all his ways, and holy in all his works. - **Psalm 145:17 (KJV)**

CHAPTER 5 - IS GOD EVIL? IS GOD AN EVILDOER?

And he said unto him, Why callest thou me good? <u>there is none good but one, *that is*, God</u>: but if thou wilt enter into life, keep the commandments. - **Matthew 19:17 (KJV)**

And Jesus said unto him, Why callest thou me good? <u>*there is* none good but one, *that is*, God</u>. - **Mark 10:18 (KJV)**

And Jesus said unto him, Why callest thou me good? <u>none *is* good, save one, *that is*, God</u>. - **Luke 18:19 (KJV)**

<u>*As for* God, his way *is* perfect</u>: the word of the Lord is tried: he *is* a buckler to all those that trust in him. - **Psalm 18:30 (KJV)**

<u>For thou *art* not a God that hath pleasure in wickedness: neither shall evil dwell with thee.</u> - **Psalm 5:4 (KJV)**

To shew that the Lord *is* upright: *he is* my rock, <u>and *there is* no unrighteousness in him</u>. - **Psalm 92:15 (KJV)**

What shall we say then? <u>*Is there* unrighteousness with God? God forbid.</u> - **Romans 9:14 (KJV)**

God has said it, and that settles it. The Bible unequivocally affirms the goodness of God. There is no evil, sin, and moral wickedness in God, for He is the embodiment of moral goodness (1 John 1:5), and the Source of all good things (James 1:17; Psalm 84:11; Psalm 104:10-31; Lamentations 3:22-23; Matthew 5:45). God's goodness is so transcendent, He cannot be tempted with evil (James 1:13), and could never conceive of engaging in sin and moral wickedness (Job 34:10). Creating evil has never changed or compromised the goodness of God. He has always been, remains and will forever be absolutely good.

IS GOD AN EVILDOER?

The answer to the question above is very interesting, because the biblical answer is both "no" and "yes". I say "no" because any time God is said to be doing evil in the Bible, it is never the evil of sin and moral wickedness, so God is not an evildoer in that sense. He will never violate His good and holy nature by doing wickedness:

> Therefore hearken unto me, ye men of understanding: <u>far be it from God, *that he should do* wickedness; and *from* the Almighty, *that he should commit* iniquity... Yea, surely God will not do wickedly,</u> neither will the Almighty pervert judgment. - **Job 34:10, 12 (KJV)**

The LORD is not a wicked evildoer in the way that sinful humanity, Satan, and demons are (Job 36:23). On the other hand, I say "yes" because there are times in the Bible where God is said to be "doing" evil, or God mentions that He will "bring about" evil, so according to Scripture, God is an "evildoer", but the evil He exercises is not a wicked expression of evil, but a righteous one.

This "righteous" evil is known as the "evil of bad outcomes", and it is a transcendent and "morally good" evil that God alone wields; when it is contemplated or exercised by God, it is always the rightful application of His justice against sin, or His producing of bad outcomes in a sinful world. There are two kinds of evil shown in the Bible, and you can determine which evil is being referred to based on its surrounding context in Scripture.

The first kind of evil is the "evil of sin and moral wickedness", which is always being displayed and exercised by sinful creatures (i.e. Satan, Adam, Ahab, Judas, etc.), and serves as an indictment to our moral corruption. The second kind of evil is the evil of bad outcomes, which is only exercised by God, and serves as the highlight of His righteousness and holiness. When the proper context is accounted for, there is nowhere in Scripture that God is morally unjustified in exercising His righteous evil:

> And the LORD repented of the evil which he thought to do unto his people. - **Exodus 32:14 (KJV)**

In the context above, God sought to destroy the Israelites for building the golden calf, and engaging in gross idolatry and revelry as they worshipped it. However, after Moses interceded for the people and entreated the LORD for mercy, God repented of the evil He intended to do (Exodus 32:1-14). When God repents, it does not mean He was guilty of some moral violation, but it simply means He is *relenting* in exercising His righteous judgment to show mercy instead.

In the contexts below, the LORD commits to bringing His evil upon the Israelites for forsaking His law, and seeking after other gods:

> The LORD shall send upon thee cursing, vexation, and rebuke, in all that thou settest thine hand unto for to do, until thou be destroyed, and until thou perish quickly; because of the wickedness of thy doings, whereby thou hast forsaken me. - **Deuteronomy 28:20 (KJV)**

> Therefore it shall come to pass, *that* as all good things are come upon you, which the LORD your God promised you; so shall the LORD bring upon you all evil things, until he have destroyed you from off this good land which the LORD your God hath given you. - **Joshua 23:15 (KJV)**

> Whithersoever they went out, the hand of the LORD was against them for evil, as the LORD had said, and as the LORD had sworn unto them: and they were greatly distressed. - **Judges 2:15 (KJV)**

As you can see, the LORD executes His righteous evil against unfaithful covenant-breakers (Deuteronomy 28:14-68; Joshua 23:6-16; Judges 2:11-15). In the age of Israel's kings, we see the evil of bad outcomes plague certain kings in various instances. We begin with King Saul, who God tormented with an evil spirit:

> But the Spirit of the LORD departed from Saul, and an evil spirit from the LORD troubled him. - **1 Samuel 16:14 (KJV)**

God sent an evil spirit to torment Saul as punishment for his sin; after Saul disobeyed the LORD, God stripped Saul of his kingship over Israel, and gave it to David (1 Samuel 15:10-35). God also used this affliction to cause the anointed, soon-to-be-king David to join Saul's royal administration (1 Samuel 16:12-23). Speaking of David, God promised to work evil against David for his sins as king:

> Thus saith the LORD, Behold, I will raise up evil against thee out of thine own house, and I will take thy wives before thine eyes, and give *them* unto thy neighbour, and he shall lie with thy wives in the sight of this sun. - **2 Samuel 12:11 (KJV)**

In the passage above, God sent Nathan the prophet to speak to King David, and pronounced evil over David's house after he committed adultery with Uriah's wife, Bathsheba, and killed Uriah to hide his sin (2 Samuel 12:1-15). This evil was fulfilled

CHAPTER 5 - IS GOD EVIL? IS GOD AN EVILDOER?

through David's son, Absalom, who slept with David's concubines to spite his father and gain political power (2 Samuel 16:20-23). After David's superfluous census, God again brought evil tidings upon Israel because of David's sin:

> <u>And when the angel stretched out his hand upon Jerusalem to destroy it, the LORD repented him of the evil, and said to the angel that destroyed the people, It is enough: stay now thine hand.</u> And the angel of the LORD was by the threshingplace of Araunah the Jebusite. - **2 Samuel 24:16 (KJV)**

Moving beyond the reigns of Saul, David, and Solomon, we enter the era of Israel's two divided kingdoms, where God sets His sights on Jeroboam, the acting king for the northern kingdom of Israel, who incited idolatry among his people, and persisted in his idolatry and irreverence after being warned:

> <u>Therefore, behold, I will bring evil upon the house of Jeroboam,</u> and will cut off from Jeroboam him that pisseth against the wall, *and* him that is shut up and left in Israel, and will take away the remnant of the house of Jeroboam, as a man taketh away dung, till it be all gone. - **1 Kings 14:10 (KJV)**

God requites Jeroboam's wicked evil with His righteous evil. Like Jeroboam, the LORD would execute judgment upon King Ahab after he was complicit in Naboth's death:

> <u>Behold, I will bring evil upon thee,</u> and will take away thy posterity, and will cut off from Ahab him that pisseth against the wall, and him that is shut up and left in Israel, - **1 Kings 21:21 (KJV)**

In the southern kingdom of Judah, as a result of the successive idolatry amongst their kings and people, God declared the future captivity of Babylon (2 Kings 21:12; 2 Chronicles 34:24), and the book of Jeremiah consistently reiterates God bringing this evil to pass (Jeremiah 4:6; Jeremiah 6:19; Jeremiah 16:10; Jeremiah 18:1-12; Jeremiah 19:3, 15; Jeremiah 21:10; Jeremiah 25:29; Jeremiah 32:42; Jeremiah 35:17; Jeremiah 36:3, 31; Jeremiah 44:2-6, 23). As Daniel prayed and sought deliverance from the 70-year, Babylonian captivity, he acknowledged the righteousness and justice of God in the evil He unleashed:

> As *it is* written in the law of Moses, all this evil is come upon us: yet made we not our prayer before the LORD our God, that we might turn from our iniquities, and understand thy truth. Therefore hath the LORD watched upon the evil, and brought it upon us: for the LORD our God *is* righteous in all his works which he doeth: for we obeyed not his voice. - **Daniel 9:13-14 (KJV)**

God exercises His righteous evil to punish evildoers, but the evil of bad outcomes does not only involve punishing sin, but also includes God producing negative outcomes as a *general* judgment as a result of sin:

> Shall a trumpet be blown in the city, and the people not be afraid? shall there be evil in a city, and the LORD hath not done *it*? - **Amos 3:6 (KJV)**

Because of sin, humanity and creation are under a curse, and with this curse, we are subject to the adverse circumstances that comes with living in a sinful world. Death, misery, loss, war, calamity, disasters, affliction, distress, and trials are among the adversities we must face from living in a fallen world. None of these adversities are sinful in and of themselves, so God uses these circumstances to bring His righteous judgment upon sinners under the curse of sin, and as Amos 3:6 states, there is no adversity or tragedy that comes to pass in our world which God has not ordained. If we are subject to these bad outcomes, we cannot ball our fist up at God, and blame Him for doing something sinful against us. As hard as it is, we must take the way of Job when bad things seem to happen out of nowhere:

> But he said unto her, Thou speakest as one of the foolish women speaketh. <u>What? shall we receive good at the hand of God, and shall we not receive evil? In all this did not Job sin with his lips.</u> - **Job 2:10 (KJV)**

After Job's tragedy and losses, from his earthly and finite perspective, Job did not know why he was suffering, but he rightly recognized these afflictions and bad outcomes were of the LORD, and the Bible affirmed the truth of this statement, for in all that Job said, he did not "sin with his lips".

Punishing evil and sin is not always the sole end of God's righteous judgment, but the LORD may exercise the evil of bad outcomes to test us like Job was, and use the adversity to bring our eyes to heaven, make us more dependent on God, help us see our sins, and further conform us into the image and likeness of Jesus Christ (Deuteronomy 8:2; Judges 3:1-4; Lamentations 3:37-42; Job 10:2; Job 34:31-32; Ecclesiastes 7:14; Romans 8:28, 35-39; 1 Peter 4:12-16; James 1:2-4; Romans 5:3-5).

And so doth God sometimes burn up our comforts to make our hidden sins run out; and then He enables us to knock them on the head and get rid of them. That may be the reason of your trial, to put an end to some long-fostered sin. It may be, too, that in this way God would prevent some future sin, some sin hidden from thine own eyes into which thou wouldst soon fall if it were not for His troubling thee by His providence. - **Charles H. Spurgeon**

Under the evil of bad outcomes, God is calling us to endure and be faithful to Him under the adversity, for righteousness will always be to our benefit, while murmuring and sinful disobedience will work towards our detriment, as Elihu told Job (Job 35:1-8). It is easier said than done, but these adversities teach us to suffer well under trial, and show us that God's grace is sufficient to sustain us in the trial (2 Corinthians 12:7-10).

You might ask, "If God doesn't actually do evil, why would God use the word 'evil' to define His actions in Scripture?" While God does no evil, He humbles Himself by calling it evil to condescend to our understanding. Further context shows that the evil God does and brings is not the moral wickedness and sin of mankind, but God doing what He pleases, and executing justice upon a creation that deserves nothing from Him. What we perceive to be evil from God is truly justice directed to men. What we interpret as evil in our earthly plane is heavenly justice as it descends from God's hand. All in all, God is not evil, nor is He an evildoer in the moral sense. We serve a good God.

From that *time* many of his disciples went back, and walked no more with him. Then said Jesus unto the twelve, Will ye also go away? Then Simon Peter answered him, Lord, to whom shall we go? thou hast the words of eternal life. And we believe and are sure that thou art that Christ, the Son of the living God.

JOHN 6:66-69 (KJV)

Each mighty power of evil
How doth the Lord assail?
'Gainst world and flesh and devil
How doth the Lord prevail?
How doth the Strength supernal
Come down into the fight?
How dost Thou, King eternal,
Win victory for the right?

Some mighty man Thou fillest
With holy hate of wrong;
Some tender soul Thou thrillest
With yearnings sweet and strong;
This woe he must diminish,
This wrong he must o'erthrow,
This warfare he must finish,
This evil power lay low.

The strength by Thee conferrèd
To others he imparts;
The fire within him stirrèd
Doth kindle other hearts:
By glowing souls attended
He rushed on the foe;
The right is well defended,
The evil power laid low.

That army, Lord, Thou leadest,
That warfare Thou dost share;
That victory Thou speedest,
The Lord of hosts is there.
Then send the Spirit fervent,
The fire that never fails;
To lighten each true servant,
Until Thy cause prevails.

Thomas H. Gill

CHAPTER 6
Evil Is In God's Good Hands

> From that *time* many of his disciples went back, and walked no more with him. Then said Jesus unto the twelve, Will ye also go away? Then Simon Peter answered him, Lord, to whom shall we go? thou hast the words of eternal life. And we believe and are sure that thou art that Christ, the Son of the living God.
> **John 6:66-69 (KJV)**

For the final time, I'll restate my thesis: God created evil, but no one wants to give Him the credit. According to the Bible, God created evil, and though He created evil, God is still good. Evil showcases the goodness and purposes of God, while working towards the Christian's ultimate good. Evil was created for God's glory, and it is why He deserves the credit, for God Himself wants the credit for evil's creation. Evil is in good hands — in God's good hands.

By the grace of God, I've tried to go above and beyond to biblically prove the veracity of my thesis. Even with the abundance of biblical proof presented, God creating evil is an idea that is difficult for many Christians to accept, for it will lead to a seismic paradigm shift, and cause us to revisit our current understanding on the things we believe about God, and challenge the presuppositions we have about ourselves and the world we live in. It is what the Bible would qualify as a "hard saying", which are statements in Scripture that naturally offend us, and cause us to reevaluate ourselves and our thinking in some way.

The hardest thing about hard sayings is while they are hard to accept, these hard sayings are no less true, and them being hard to accept does not diminish our responsibility to wholly accept these sayings *as* truth.

> Great peace have they which love thy law: <u>and nothing shall offend them.</u> - **Psalm 119:165 (KJV)**

We are called to be conformed to God's truth through the renewing of our mind, even though His truth may be offensive to our natural minds (Romans 12:2; Psalm 119:165). Nothing in Scripture should offend us, and that includes the hard sayings (Matthew 11:6; Luke 7:23).

If we despise what the Bible says, and reject it because it offends us in some way, then the problem is with us, not with God and His Word, and we ought to repent of our hardheartedness, and seek for God's Word to dwell richly in us, reform our minds, and transform us to be Christians who will readily receive the whole counsel of God (Hebrews 4:12; Colossians 3:16; Psalm 51:10; Psalm 119:32-34; Jeremiah 31:33-34; Hebrews 8:10-11; Ezekiel 36:26-27; Proverbs 3:1-8; Acts 17:10-12). Offence towards Scripture can rob of us great blessing; rejecting what God says can have temporal and eternal implications, and I want to focus in on a passage in Scripture to illustrate this point.

TO WHOM SHALL WE GO?

Our story occurs at some point during Jesus Christ's earthly ministry. After Jesus fed the 5,000 and declared Himself to be the Bread of Life from heaven, His hearers wondered how He Himself could be literal bread for them to eat (John 6:52), so Christ decides to drop a bombshell to offend their minds:

CHAPTER 6 - EVIL IS IN GOD'S GOOD HANDS

> Then Jesus said unto them, Verily, verily, I say unto you, <u>Except ye eat the flesh of the Son of man, and drink his blood, ye have no life in you. Whoso eateth my flesh, and drinketh my blood, hath eternal life;</u> and I will raise him up at the last day. <u>For my flesh is meat indeed, and my blood is drink indeed. He that eateth my flesh, and drinketh my blood, dwelleth in me, and I in him.</u> As the living Father hath sent me, and I live by the Father: <u>so he that eateth me, even he shall live by me.</u> This is that bread which came down from heaven: not as your fathers did eat manna, and are dead: <u>he that eateth of this bread shall live for ever.</u> These things said he in the synagogue, as he taught in Capernaum. - **John 6:53-59 (KJV)**

After this statement, those in the synagogue of Capernaum could not believe what they were hearing. From their natural minds, they believed Jesus was encouraging cannibalism in requiring them to literally eat His flesh and drink His blood. From their carnal perspective, they were thinking Jesus was encouraging them violate Scripture itself, for in the law of Moses, drinking the blood of any creature was forbidden (Genesis 9:2-4; Leviticus 17:10-14), and eating human flesh was the sinful expression of being cursed by God (Deuteronomy 28:52-57; 2 Kings 6:24-33). Because Christ's spiritual words offended their natural minds, and attacked their cultural and religious sensibilities, the Jews which followed Him could not accept Jesus' words:

> Many therefore of his disciples, when they had heard *this*, said, <u>This is an hard saying; who can hear it?</u> When Jesus knew in himself that his disciples murmured at it, he said unto them, <u>Doth this offend you?</u> - **John 6:60-61 (KJV)**

As they naturally understood it, what Jesus put forth was a hard saying which they could not receive. However, Jesus was not speaking about eating His literal flesh or drinking His literal blood; being a *physical* partaker of these things will not confer salvation or eternal life to any man.

Christ is talking about spiritually eating, or being a *spiritual* partaker in His flesh and blood, which is the body and blood that establishes the new covenant in Christ, and is given up for our redemption (Matthew 26:26-28; Mark 14:22-24; Luke 22:19-20; Hebrews 12:24). This was laid out plainly by Jesus at the Lord's Supper, and reinforced by Apostle Paul when implementing communion, which is a symbolic reminder of Christ's literal death, and the spiritual effects produced from it (1 Corinthians 11:23-26).

When we receive the gospel, and are regenerated by the Holy Spirit, we become spiritual partakers and recipients of the things that make our salvation effectual, which is the atonement made with Jesus' broken body and shed blood. We don't need to physically eat anything to make this happen; we automatically become spiritual partakers of Christ once we come under the new covenant established by Him.

If the hearers had this spiritual understanding, they would have not considered Christ's words to be a hard saying, and would not have been offended in the way that they were. But because Jesus' words were spiritual in nature, they couldn't apprehend them with their natural minds, for they must be spiritually discerned (1 Corinthians 2:9-14; Matthew 13:10-17; John 6:63-65; Isaiah 6:9-10; Isaiah 64:4; Proverbs 20:12).

They could not follow on because they were using their natural minds to receive God's spiritual words. As a result, they became offended by the hard saying, and many of Christ's following turned away from Him:

> From that *time* many of his disciples went back, and walked no more with him. Then said Jesus unto the twelve, Will ye also go away? - **John 6:66–67 (KJV)**

After the mass exodus, Christ turns to His twelve disciples, and inquires whether they will also forsake Him for His teaching, but Peter speaks up on the disciples' behalf, and offers a revolutionary and spiritually mature answer:

> Then Simon Peter answered him, Lord, to whom shall we go? thou hast the words of eternal life. And we believe and are sure that thou art that Christ, the Son of the living God. - **John 6:68–69 (KJV)**

What an answer! Notice that Peter and the disciples did not tell Christ whether they were offended by His hard saying, for even if they were, it did not matter. The twelve gave up everything to follow Christ, and Jesus assured them they would inherit eternal life, and regain abundantly more than they lost for their faithfulness (Matthew 19:27-30; Luke 18:28-30). Save Judas, the disciples believed that Jesus Christ was the Son of God, and possessed the words that could give and bring about eternal life.

Compared to eternal life, where else could they go? Where else would they *want* to go? Outside of Christ, they had no other Hope, and they had no better Hope. So even if these words offended their natural minds, even if they didn't understand the spiritual significance of His hard sayings, they would still *follow* Christ. They would still *love* Christ. They would still *trust* Christ. This momentary offence would not dissuade them. And because they pressed on despite being offended, eleven of these twelve went on to turn the world upside down for the sake of the gospel (Acts 17:6-7). I'm sure the disciples are eternally grateful they did not forsake Christ.

When contrasted to the response of the twelve disciples, those who forsook Christ in this moment should be viewed as a tragedy. They forfeited a great opportunity for blessing and growth because they couldn't get past being offended by God's Word. We are not aware of the fate of these disciples, but we do know they "walked no more with him" (John 6:66). If they never returned back to Christ in their lifetimes, the eternal implications would be catastrophic. Don't let your offence *to* Scripture rob you of the blessing that comes *through* Scripture. Hard sayings and all, humble yourself under the mighty hand of God, and He will exalt you and bless you — in this life, or in the next (1 Peter 5:6).

God Created Evil — To Whom Shall Ye Go?
Hopefully, you acknowledge that God created evil. In the face of this hard saying, will you still follow Him? Will you still love Him? Will you still trust Him? I say this because there are some immature Christians who would hear this truth, and may become offended by it. There are some immature Christians who might be offended with God because of this truth. And God forbid, there might be some professing Christians that will forsake Christ altogether because of this truth. They will allow offence to consume them, and they will forget Psalm 119:165.

But for my offended Christians, I ask you this — in your anger and apostasy against God, to whom shall *ye* go? What benefit is there to be angry at God, or what profit is to be found in forsaking Him? God is going to be God whether you *agree* with Him or not. God is going to be God whether you *believe* in Him or not. God is going to be God whether you *love* Him or not. His Word is not going to change to accommodate your feelings, and forsaking God will only bring hurt to your own soul. Nothing about this truth diminishes God's role as the Saviour; Christ will still be the way, the truth, and the life for sinners (John 14:6). If you walk in persistent rebellion, you may die in your sins (Luke 13:3; 1 John 2:19; 1 John 3:6-10). The unstoppable force of your offended ego will one day meet the Immovable Object which is God, and you will *always* be on the losing end of that battle:

> Woe unto him that striveth with his Maker! *Let* the potsherd *strive* with the potsherds of the earth. Shall the clay say to him that fashioneth it, What makest thou? or thy work, He hath no hands? - **Isaiah 45:9 (KJV)**

Why strive with God or contend with your Maker? God created evil. It may be hard to accept, but that is what it is. Instead of letting go, hold fast to Christ all the more, for He is our only Hope in the midst of this sobering truth. We may not agree with it, we may not fully understand why, but we will still love and trust Christ in spite of it.

Sometimes, the LORD will offend our minds to reveal our hearts. These hard sayings may be the way to test our love for God, and refine our love for God, for loving God is the greatest commandment and ought to be our highest aim:

> Jesus said unto him, Thou shalt love the Lord thy God with all thy heart, and with all thy soul, and with all thy mind. This is the first and great commandment. - **Matthew 22:37-38 (KJV)**

Consider this analogy on biblical love: Love is cultivated and expressed in varying degrees. Think about the ways your love for someone has developed and deepened throughout your own life. Our love usually begins as babes in the womb and at birth — we become familiar with our mother, and recognize that she has been our source of sustenance in the womb, and is our source of sustenance at the breast. She provides us with attention, emotional comfort, and is the one who primarily looks to our well-being around the clock (Isaiah 49:15). As a result, we first love her for what she does for us; her benevolence towards us is the first to court and captivate our affections.

There's nothing wrong with loving someone for what they've done. But that is the beginning and the shallow end of love. It is natural and customary to begin love this way, as this is how most of our customary relationships are formed (i.e. parents, siblings, grandparents). We don't know enough about the object of our love to love them for who they are. That comes with time. In most cases, the things someone does is a proxy for who they are. As a biblical parallel, at first, we love God because He first loved us, and sent Christ to die for our sins so we could be reconciled to God, and inherit eternal life (1 John 4:10, 19; Romans 5:8-10; John 3:16; Ephesians 2:4-9; Psalm 31:23; Psalm 68:19; Psalm 103:1-6; Psalm 116:1-8; Deuteronomy 7:6-8).

Over time, the next level to love is loving someone for who they are. You can see the beauty and excellencies of their character, appreciate them, and are moved to align and devote yourself to them. You've probably experienced this at some point in time with your parents, and it is the same with God — as we learn more about Him in the Scriptures, we begin to see more of His excellent and awesome character, which results in us loving God for who He is (Psalm 8:1; Psalm 36:5-9; Psalm 42:1-4; Psalm 63:1-6; Psalm 73:25-26; Psalm 84:1-2, 10; Psalm 148:13; Matthew 26:6-13; Mark 14:3-9; John 12:1-8; Luke 7:36-50).

The highest form of love is loving someone *in spite* of who they are or what they've done. They may possess toxic traits, or have good traits that offend your sinful and ignorant sensibilities, but even with that in the picture, you aim to love them (see their highest good) to the uttermost. You may have also reached this point with your parents, your children, or with your spouse in marriage. Even with their flaws or your contentions with them, you make the intentional choice to love them all the same. The righteous virtue of your love is put on display, for it is not a natural way to love, but is evidence of the supernatural love of God at work in us:

> Ye have heard that it hath been said, Thou shalt love thy neighbour, and hate thine enemy. But I say unto you, Love your enemies, bless them that curse you, do good to them that hate you, and pray for them which despitefully use you, and persecute you; That ye may be the children of your Father which is in heaven: for he maketh his sun to rise on the evil and on the good, and sendeth rain on the just and on the unjust. For if ye love them which love you, what reward have ye? do not even the publicans the same? And if ye salute your brethren only, what do ye more *than others*? do not even the publicans so? Be ye therefore perfect, even as your Father which is in heaven is perfect. - **Matthew 5:43-48 (KJV)**

This is the pinnacle of biblical love, and herein is God's love being perfected in us (Matthew 5:48; Luke 23:34; Acts 7:60; 1 John 3:16-19). If this is what is owed to your evil enemies who hate you, or people you are not in agreement with, or people who have wronged you, how much more is this kind of love owed to God, who has *never* wronged you, and seeks your ultimate good in saving your soul? We owe God our ultimate affection, allegiance and fealty. We have no right to be offended with God, for He has not given us any reason to question Him, or put in Him on trial (Job 33:13; Job 34:16-19, 23; Job 35:2).

If we are offended with God's Word, we need to examine ourselves and reassess our love for God; the hard sayings in Scripture are the nexus point where we will either regress in our love, or be refined in our love for God. Don't let unbelief prevail, and cause you to run into the jaws of Satan because you think God is a hard master, and are unwilling to accept His words, decrees and mandates (1 Peter 5:8; Matthew 25:24-25; Hebrews 3:12; Mark 8:38; Luke 9:26). Harden not your heart at the hard saying, but incline your heart to His testimonies (Psalm 95:6-8; Psalm 119:36; Luke 11:28). For God will do wondrously for those who humbly and gladly keep His words:

> <u>He that hath my commandments, and keepeth them, he it is that loveth me: and he that loveth me shall be loved of my Father, and I will love him, and will manifest myself to him</u>... Jesus answered and said unto him, <u>If a man love me, he will keep my words: and my Father will love him, and we will come unto him, and make our abode with him.</u> - **John 14:21, 23 (KJV)**

The LORD will manifest Himself to you in His Word, and manifest Himself in your life in a remarkable way if you trust Him at His word, and keep His word without offence. Where else can we go? Our God alone has the words of eternal life, and there is nowhere else we can go without being destroyed (Psalm 73:27; Psalm 139:7). In spite of God creating evil, we will still love, trust, and follow Him to the end (Job 13:15). Take a moment to ponder this quote from Charles Spurgeon about loving the Bible:

> Yes, a true love for the great Book will bring us great peace from the great God and be a great protection to us. Let us live constantly in the society of the law of the LORD, and it

will breed in our hearts a restfulness such as nothing else can. The Holy Spirit acts as a Comforter through the Word and sheds abroad those benign influences which calm the tempests of the soul. Nothing is a stumbling block to the man who has the Word of God dwelling in him richly. He takes up his daily cross, and it becomes a delight. For the fiery trial he is prepared and counts it not strange, so as to be utterly cast down by it. He is neither stumbled by prosperity — as so many are — nor crushed by adversity — as others have been — for he lives beyond the changing circumstances of external life. When his LORD puts before him some great mystery of the faith which makes others cry, "This is an hard saying; who can hear it?" the believer accepts it without question; for his intellectual difficulties are overcome by his reverent awe of the law of the LORD, which is to him the supreme authority to which he joyfully bows. LORD, work in us this love, this peace, this rest, this day. - **Charles H. Spurgeon**

WHY DID GOD CREATE EVIL?

We are now at the point where we begin to ask, "Why?" Why *did* God create evil? What was His purpose in doing so? What could He possibly stand to gain from it? You already know the answer; I've mentioned it multiple times in my thesis, and expounded upon it in Chapter 3. Have you figured it out? God created evil for His glory.

God created evil to meet His preeminent purpose of glorifying Himself. As the self-sufficient God, He never needed to do this, but through creation, He wanted to glorify Himself out of His own good pleasure (Revelation 4:11). In Genesis 1:31, when the LORD observed His completed creation, and recognized it to be "very good", this Spirit-inspired declaration was not made simply because the universe worked in perfect harmony in the *present*, but it was also very good because creation would accomplish the *end* God intended the universe to meet — evil included. It would achieve the aim of God glorifying Himself through man's redemption, from which evil's existence and sin are the necessary prerequisites for.

Again, this was God's master plan from before the foundation of the world (Ephesians 1:3-14). Without evil, there is no adoption in Christ without a broken relationship in Adam from sin (Romans 8:14-17; Galatians 4:1-7; Colossians 1:12-13). Without evil, there is no redemption in Christ without a debt and a price to be paid from Adam's sin (Acts 20:28; Ephesians 1:14; 1 Corinthians 6:19-20; 1 Corinthians 7:23; Hebrews 9:11-12; Titus 2:13-14). Without evil, there is no forgiveness of sins in Christ without the commission of sin in Adam (Colossians 1:14; Hebrews 9:22).

And without evil and sin in the picture, God could not properly showcase the full spectrum of His perfect character, including His wrath and His power in judgment against sin and evil, which uniquely highlights His incomprehensible holiness and righteousness (Romans 9:22-24). Evil is the black ink, the negative space, and the backdrop which allows God's excellent character to shine in its fulness, and in all its bright and magnificent colours.

To paraphrase John Calvin, creation is the theater where the LORD puts His glory on display; God has made evil the villain of this story, and through evil, God has made Himself the Hero who will utterly vanquish it, to the praise of His glory. He will overcome all evil by His goodness (John 16:33; 1 John 4:4; Revelation 20:10-15; Revelation 21:1-8, 27).

It's easy to write essays on evil until you have been afflicted by it; it is easy to make evil into a philosophical, discussion topic until you have been buffeted by its many blows (Proverbs 18:14; 2 Timothy 3:12; Hebrews 11:36-38; Job 2:10). There are forms of evil and suffering that I would never want to experience in my lifetime, and I grieve for those who do, so I don't make light of this. Evil is a scourge to humanity, and there is so much evil, sin and suffering in our world (1 John 5:19), so hearing that we are subjected to evil all for God's glory may be hard to accept; it can be hard for us to accept that God would allow evil to enter our world, and subject us to evil's design with sin and death in creation. But despite the visceral hardship that evil brings, it was created to glorify God.

And before you storm the throne room of heaven, and bitterly complain to God about all the evils you've been subjected to, please remember these two things. For starters, while the LORD was sovereign in creating evil, and made it possible for evil and sin to enter our world, *we* are the ones who brought evil into the world through our disobedience (Genesis 2:17; Genesis 3:6; Romans 5:12). Adam's sin pulled the trigger, and caused all of humanity to be subjugated to the evils we now face. We are responsible for the evil and suffering that ravages our creation, not God. God is absolutely sovereign, yet man is absolutely responsible, so our haste to blame God is foolhardy.

Secondly, despite the unspeakable evils we have faced, no one has ever been subjected to more evil than God Himself in Christ. For sinners, being terrorized by sin and evil is justified because of our disobedience. However, Jesus left eternal glory to condescend to His sinful creation, and be crucified at the hands of sinful men (John 1:14; Hebrews 2:9, 16-17; Hebrews 4:14-16; Psalm 113:4-6). Jesus became sin who knew no sin as the Innocent One (2 Corinthians 5:21). Christ's death was the execution of God's divine justice, but it also marked humanity's most evil act.

Think of the grossest atrocities that have befallen men — they will *never* compare to Christ's sufferings (Philippians 2:5-8; Lamentations 1:12-13; Isaiah 40:25; Isaiah 46:5). Not even close. God seeks to have preeminence in all things, and that also includes preeminence in suffering (Colossians 1:18; Hebrews 2:10). Understanding this, how can you be mad at God for subjecting you to evil and suffering, when God subjected Himself to the *worst* evil and sufferings? What room do you have to claim being more oppressed than God in the flesh? The LORD is so invested in delivering us from evil, He joined us in our miry evil to liberate His people. If God created evil for His glory, there should be no complaints from us (Isaiah 45:9; Ecclesiates 8:4; Daniel 4:35; Job 34:33).

WHAT EVIL MEANS FOR US

Evil has a role in glorifying God, but it also has a role in edifying us as well. If God can put an end to evil, why does He allow it to persist and terrorize humanity? Why doesn't He end evil's reign right now? What good does evil have in staying around? Well, we can find our answer to these questions in the book of Judges, but we first need to establish a little bit of backstory.

After the death of Moses, Joshua and the Israelites began to inherit the Promised Land (Canaan) through battle and conquest (Joshua 1:1-6; Joshua 11:23; Joshua 21:43-45; Genesis 15:17-21). By the time Joshua was about die, Israel conquered a majority of Canaan, but each tribe of Israel was now responsible for completing their conquest, and ousting the remnant of Canaanites that still existed within their divided and allotted territories (Joshua 23:1-13).

Once we enter the age of judges in the book of Judges, and Israel had been established in the land for a while, God reveals that during the period of their conquests, there were nations in Canaan that He did not allow Joshua and Israel to conquer:

And the anger of the LORD was hot against Israel; and he

said, Because that this people hath transgressed my covenant which I commanded their fathers, and have not hearkened unto my voice; I also will not henceforth drive out any from before them of the nations which Joshua left when he died: That through them I may prove Israel, whether they will keep the way of the LORD to walk therein, as their fathers did keep *it*, or not. Therefore the LORD left those nations, without driving them out hastily; neither delivered he them into the hand of Joshua. - **Judges 2:20-23 (KJV)**

This revelation comes through a proclamation of judgment against Israel for their compromise and idolatry; however, it also reveals God's foresight of Israel's sins (Deuteronomy 31:16-18), and how He made preparations to chastise Israel for the sins they *would* commit, and test their faithfulness to God in the midst of these chastisements. The unconquered Canaanite nations were left to punish and prove God's people.

But there was a greater reason behind these unconquered nations remaining with Israel:

Now these *are* the nations which the LORD left, to prove Israel by them, *even* as many *of Israel* as had not known all the wars of Canaan; Only that the generations of the children of Israel might know, to teach them war, at the least such as before knew nothing thereof; *Namely*, five lords of the Philistines, and all the Canaanites, and the Sidonians, and the Hivites that dwelt in mount Lebanon, from mount Baalhermon unto the entering in of Hamath. And they were to prove Israel by them, to know whether they would hearken unto the commandments of the LORD, which he commanded their fathers by the hand of Moses. - **Judges 3:1-4 (KJV)**

Beyond judgment and punishment, God left these nations to coexist with Israel to "teach them war". At this point in history, Joshua and all his generation that were involved in the conquests of Canaan were dead, so this current generation of Israelites had not known war (Judges 2:7-10; Judges 3:1-2). Unlike the passage in Judges 2, this purpose was not contingent on their disobedience, but was focused on the edification and faithfulness of Israel, which would be needed to retain their posterity in the land against their enemies.

The LORD understood that the land which the Israelites occupied was fruitful and arable (Exodus 3:8; Numbers 13:17-27; Ezekiel 20:6), so these remnant nations would eventually seek to claim or reclaim this land and its resources for themselves. Couple this with the fact that Israel displaced these nations through their conquests, these nations one day might be inspired by envy or revenge. By teaching them to war, Israel would learn to become more dependent on God, and be better equipped to defend against invaders and encroachments. Their willingness to know war, contend with their enemies, and trust God for victory would be the only way for Israel's civil peace to be established.

Now what do these passages have to do with evil, and why it persists in our world? I think Matthew Henry provides some helpful insight on these passages:

> Israel was a figure of the church militant, that must fight its way to a triumphant state. The soldiers of Christ must endure hardness... Corruption is therefore left remaining in the hearts even of good Christians, that they may learn war, may keep on the whole armour of God, and stand continually upon their guard. - **Matthew Henry**

Evil still persists in creation because God delights in creating

CHAPTER 6 - EVIL IS IN GOD'S GOOD HANDS

battle-tested Christians. He can easily do away with evil, but God allows evil to persist so He can teach us to war against it, contend with evil in its every form, and increasingly depend on Him alone to overcome it (Psalm 18:31-39; Psalm 144:1-2; Psalm 97:10; Proverbs 8:13; Proverbs 28:4; 1 Thessalonians 5:21-22; Ephesians 5:11; Romans 12:21).

Joshua, the captain of Israel's army, subdued Canaan and spoiled its stronghold in the land; Joshua led in the decisive victories, but Israel was still responsible for continuing the conquest, going forth to battle, and destroying the remaining evils in their respective territories.

But Joshua is a type of Christ, and the conquest of Canaan is a picture of the Christian life. To a greater degree, Jesus, the Captain of our salvation, subdued the powers of evil — sin, Satan, the world, the flesh, hell, death, and the grave were spoiled by Christ's power so we could inherit eternal life. The *eternal* victory has already been won, but there are still battles we must fight to experience *temporal* triumphs in this life. There is still evil we must contend with and conquer.

> The earthly history of the Church is not a history merely of conflict with evil, but of conquest *over* evil. - **Benjamin B. Warfield**

We cannot truly appreciate eternity if all we know is the bliss of Eden our entire lives. We cannot truly appreciate the presence of the light until we experience the darkness. Yes, God has given Christians eternal life in Christ, but God also wants to make us fit for heaven by sanctifying us, enlarging our affections *for* Him, solidifying our allegiance *to* Him, and making us battle-tested along the way. Eternity is the culmination of the rigorous, sanctifying work that God begins in us as we war with evil here below (Philippians 1:6).

The LORD has struck the decisive blow, and has already secured the victory over evil (1 Corinthians 15:55-57; 2 Corinthians 2:14; Genesis 3:15; 1 John 3:8; Colossians 2:13-15; Romans 8:3-4), but God wants us to join in the present spiritual battle, and exercise ourselves in the conquest of evil, so that we can overcome it in the end, like Christ did (John 16:33; 1 John 4:4; 1 John 5:4-5; Revelation 2:7; Revelation 2:11; Revelation 2:17; Revelation 2:26; Revelation 3:5; Revelation 3:12; Revelation 3:21; Revelation 21:7).

This is why even though we become Christians, and are regenerated as new creations, God allows the flesh (our sinful nature, indwelling sin) to remain with us (Romans 7). God wants our conquest of evil to begin with the evil in ourselves, and wants us to overcome sin's power and our appetite for sin, primarily by yielding to the Spirit through prayer and Scripture, being filled with the Spirit indwelling us, and actively mortifying our flesh by the Holy Spirit's power. This daily contention with the flesh causes us to fight the sin in us, and long to be liberated from this body of death indwelt by sin:

> I find then a law, that, when I would do good, evil is present with me. For I delight in the law of God after the inward man: But I see another law in my members, warring against the law of my mind, and bringing me into captivity to the law of sin which is in my members. O wretched man that I am! who shall deliver me from the body of this death? - **Romans 7:21-24 (KJV)**

Therefore, brethren, we are debtors, not to the flesh, to live after the flesh. For if ye live after the flesh, ye shall die: but if ye through the Spirit do mortify the deeds of the body, ye shall live. For as many as are led by the Spirit of God, they are the sons of God. - **Romans 8:12-14 (KJV)**

Let not sin therefore reign in your mortal body, that ye should obey it in the lusts thereof. Neither yield ye your members *as* instruments of unrighteousness unto sin: but yield yourselves unto God, as those that are alive from the dead, and your members *as* instruments of righteousness unto God. For sin shall not have dominion over you: for ye are not under the law, but under grace. What then? shall we sin, because we are not under the law, but under grace? God forbid. Know ye not, that to whom ye yield yourselves servants to obey, his servants ye are to whom ye obey; whether of sin unto death, or of obedience unto righteousness? - **Romans 6:12-16 (KJV)**

But put ye on the Lord Jesus Christ, and make not provision for the flesh, to *fulfil* the lusts *thereof*. - **Romans 13:14 (KJV)**

Dearly beloved, I beseech *you* as strangers and pilgrims, abstain from fleshly lusts, which war against the soul; - **1 Peter 2:11 (KJV)**

Wherefore be ye not unwise, but understanding what the will of the Lord *is*. And be not drunk with wine, wherein is excess; but be filled with the Spirit; Speaking to yourselves in psalms and hymns and spiritual songs, singing and making melody in your heart to the Lord; Giving thanks always for all things unto God and the Father in the name of our Lord Jesus Christ; - **Ephesians 5:17-20 (KJV)**

This I say then, Walk in the Spirit, and ye shall not fulfil the lust of the flesh. For the flesh lusteth against the Spirit, and the Spirit against the flesh: and these are contrary the one to the other: so that ye cannot do the things that ye would...

And they that are Christ's have crucified the flesh with the affections and lusts. If we live in the Spirit, let us also walk in the Spirit. - **Galatians 5:16–17, 24–25 (KJV)**

Know ye not that they which run in a race run all, but one receiveth the prize? So run, that ye may obtain. And every man that striveth for the mastery is temperate in all things. Now they *do it* to obtain a corruptible crown; but we an incorruptible. I therefore so run, not as uncertainly; so fight I, not as one that beateth the air: But I keep under my body, and bring *it* into subjection: lest that by any means, when I have preached to others, I myself should be a castaway. - **1 Corinthians 9:24–27 (KJV)**

But refuse profane and old wives' fables, and exercise thyself *rather* unto godliness. For bodily exercise profiteth little: but godliness is profitable unto all things, having promise of the life that now is, and of that which is to come. - **1 Timothy 4:7–8 (KJV)**

Sin is an enemy. It is compared to a "serpent" (Prov. xxiii. 32). It has four stings — shame, guilt, horror, death. Will a man love that which seeks his death? Surely then it is better to love God than sin. - **Thomas Watson**

It is we that are to mortify the deeds of the flesh. It is our duty, but of ourselves we cannot do it; it must be done in or by the Spirit. - **John Owen**

That the choicest believers, who are assuredly freed from the condemning power of sin, ought yet to make it their business all their days to mortify the indwelling power of sin. - **John Owen**

We mortify sin by cherishing the principle of holiness and sanctification in our souls, labouring to increase and strengthen it by growing in grace, and by a constancy and frequency in acting of it in all duties, on all occasions, abounding in the fruits of it. - **John Owen**

The propensities of fallen nature are not eradicated in the children of God, though by grace they are made partakers of a new principle, which enables them, in the Lord's strength, to resist and mortify the body of sin, so that it cannot reign in them. - **John Newton**

If you do not die to sin, you shall die for sin. If you do not slay sin, sin will slay you. - **Charles H. Spurgeon**

We must slay the evil within ourselves by God's grace. Our striving with evil is why we remain in the world, for we must forsake it to prove our love and allegiance to our LORD, setting our affections on things above, and hoping that as we are estranged from the world, we will one day be at home in a better country, and find rest in the eternal city, whose Builder and Maker is God:

<u>Again, the devil taketh him up into an exceeding high mountain, and sheweth him all the kingdoms of the world, and the glory of them;</u> And saith unto him, All these things will I give thee, if thou wilt fall down and worship me. Then saith Jesus unto him, Get thee hence, Satan: <u>for it is written, Thou shalt worship the Lord thy God, and him only shalt thou serve.</u> - **Matthew 4:8-10 (KJV)**

Thou shalt have no other gods before me. - **Exodus 20:3 (KJV)**

Then said Jesus unto his disciples, If any *man* will come after me, let him deny himself, and take up his cross, and follow me. For whosoever will save his life shall lose it: and whosoever will lose his life for my sake shall find it. For what is a man profited, if he shall gain the whole world, and lose his own soul? or what shall a man give in exchange for his soul? - **Matthew 16:24–26 (KJV)**

So when they had dined, Jesus saith to Simon Peter, Simon, *son* of Jonas, lovest thou me more than these? He saith unto him, Yea, Lord; thou knowest that I love thee. He saith unto him, Feed my lambs. - **John 21:15 (KJV)**

I have given them thy word; and the world hath hated them, because they are not of the world, even as I am not of the world. I pray not that thou shouldest take them out of the world, but that thou shouldest keep them from the evil. They are not of the world, even as I am not of the world. - **John 17:14–16 (KJV)**

And be not conformed to this world: but be ye transformed by the renewing of your mind, that ye may prove what *is* that good, and acceptable, and perfect, will of God. - **Romans 12:2 (KJV)**

Ye adulterers and adulteresses, know ye not that the friendship of the world is enmity with God? whosoever therefore will be a friend of the world is the enemy of God. - **James 4:4 (KJV)**

By faith Moses, when he was come to years, refused to be called the son of Pharaoh's daughter; Choosing rather to suffer affliction with the people of God, than to enjoy the pleasures of sin for a season; Esteeming the reproach of Christ greater riches than the treasures in Egypt: for he had respect unto the recompence of the reward. - **Hebrews 11:24-26 (KJV)**

Love not the world, neither the things *that are* in the world. If any man love the world, the love of the Father is not in him. For all that *is* in the world, the lust of the flesh, and the lust of the eyes, and the pride of life, is not of the Father, but is of the world. And the world passeth away, and the lust thereof: but he that doeth the will of God abideth for ever. - **1 John 2:15-17 (KJV)**

But what things were gain to me, those I counted loss for Christ. Yea doubtless, and I count all things *but* loss for the excellency of the knowledge of Christ Jesus my Lord: for whom I have suffered the loss of all things, and do count them *but* dung, that I may win Christ, - **Philippians 3:7-8 (KJV)**

Pure religion and undefiled before God and the Father is this, To visit the fatherless and widows in their affliction, *and* to keep himself unspotted from the world. - **James 1:27 (KJV)**

May the LORD keep you unspotted from the world. You shall overcome by the blood of the Lamb. - **George Whitefield**

Christ is not loved at all if not loved above all. - **Charles H. Spurgeon**

It is better to be a pattern of holiness, than a partner in

wickedness. It is better to go to heaven with a few, than to hell in the crowd. We must walk in an opposite course to the men of the world. - **Thomas Watson**

How can those men see a holy God who love unholy things? - **Charles H. Spurgeon**

We must spurn the allure of evil in the world, and cultivate our appetites for heaven. Our striving with evil is why we are not invulnerable to Satan and his kingdom of darkness, for he is the god of this world, whose influence pervades the children of disobedience, and who sets himself up as the adversary of Christ and His church. Along with his hordes of demons, Satan seeks to keep men in sin and bondage, and devour the saints who are at liberty in the world. As the Father of all spirits, God wants the joint-heirs of Christ to acquaint themselves with the unseen realm, and recognize that our true battle is spiritual in nature:

> Finally, my brethren, be strong in the Lord, and in the power of his might. <u>Put on the whole armour of God, that ye may be able to stand against the wiles of the devil. For we wrestle not against flesh and blood, but against principalities, against powers, against the rulers of the darkness of this world, against spiritual wickedness in high places.</u> Wherefore take unto you the whole armour of God, that ye may be able to withstand in the evil day, and having done all, to stand. - **Ephesians 6:10-13 (KJV)**

> And the God of peace shall bruise Satan under your feet shortly. The grace of our Lord Jesus Christ *be* with you. Amen. - **Romans 16:20 (KJV)**

CHAPTER 6 - EVIL IS IN GOD'S GOOD HANDS

Submit yourselves therefore to God. <u>Resist the devil, and he will flee from you.</u> - **James 4:7 (KJV)**

<u>Be sober, be vigilant; because your adversary the devil, as a roaring lion, walketh about, seeking whom he may devour: Whom resist stedfast in the faith, knowing that the same afflictions are accomplished in your brethren that are in the world.</u> But the God of all grace, who hath called us unto his eternal glory by Christ Jesus, <u>after that ye have suffered a while, make you perfect, stablish, strengthen, settle *you*</u>. To him *be* glory and dominion for ever and ever. Amen. - **1 Peter 5:8–11 (KJV)**

Ye are of God, little children, and have overcome them: <u>because greater is he that is in you, than he that is in the world.</u> - **1 John 4:4 (KJV)**

Consider the end of any temptation; this is Satan's end and sin's end,—that is, the dishonour of God and the ruin of our souls. - **John Owen**

There is one great master power of evil who is called, "your adversary the devil," but there are also multitudes of demons under his control who are all, like himself, full of hatred to God and to goodness and bent upon doing as much harm as they can to the Kingdom of Christ among men. We do not know how numerous these evil spirits are, but there is reason to believe that there are very many of them, so that it will be no easy task to overcome them—and it is no wonder that there is so much evil in the world when there are so many evil spirits constantly seeking to lead men astray. - **Charles H. Spurgeon**

There is no believer in Christ, no follower of that which is true and lovely, and of good repute, who will not find himself, at some season or other, attacked by this foul fiend and the legions enlisted in his service. Now, behold your adversary. Yea, though ye cannot see his face, or detect his form, believe that such a foe withstands you. It is not a myth, nor a dream, nor a superstitious imagination. He is as real a being as ourselves. Though a spirit, he has as much real power over hearts as we have over the hearts of others; nay, in many cases far more. This is, I repeat it, no vision of the night; no phantom of a disordered brain. That wicked one is as sternly real this day as when Christ met him in deadly conflict in the wilderness of temptation. Believers now have to fight with Apollyon in the valley of Humiliation. Woe to the professors of godliness who are defeated by this deadly antagonist; they will find it a terrible reality in the world to come. Against this prince of darkness we utter afresh this morning the warning of the apostle, "Whom resist stedfast in the faith." - **Charles H. Spurgeon**

So, Christian, I bid you again to look at your great adversary, that you may realize how stern is the conflict in which you are engaged. You are often afraid of Satan, but he is never afraid of you. If you turn your back in the day of battle, it is not likely that he will turn his. If you are to come off more than conqueror in this lifelong fight, you must be no mere feather-bed soldier. - **Charles H. Spurgeon**

We must resist the scourge of Satan, and engage the kingdom of darkness with the marvellous light of the LORD. Lastly, our strivings with evil is why we are continually faced with trials, afflictions, temptations, troubles, and tribulations, for our sufferings humble us, cause us to depend on God's sufficient grace and peace, and make us more like the Lord Jesus Christ who Himself suffered, which prepares us for the inconceivable glory that awaits those who endure these sufferings:

Though he were a Son, yet learned he obedience by the things which he suffered; And being made perfect, he became the author of eternal salvation unto all them that obey him; - **Hebrews 5:8-9 (KJV)**

The Spirit itself beareth witness with our spirit, that we are the children of God: And if children, then heirs; heirs of God, and joint-heirs with Christ; if so be that we suffer with him, that we may be also glorified together. For I reckon that the sufferings of this present time *are* not worthy *to be compared* with the glory which shall be revealed in us. - **Romans 8:16-18 (KJV)**

But we have this treasure in earthen vessels, that the excellency of the power may be of God, and not of us. *We are* troubled on every side, yet not distressed; *we are* perplexed, but not in despair; Persecuted, but not forsaken; cast down, but not destroyed... For which cause we faint not; but though our outward man perish, yet the inward *man* is renewed day by day. For our light affliction, which is but for a moment, worketh for us a far more exceeding *and* eternal weight of glory; - **2 Corinthians 4:7-9, 16-17 (KJV)**

Many *are* the afflictions of the righteous: but the LORD delivereth him out of them all. - **Psalm 34:19 (KJV)**

Beloved, think it not strange concerning the fiery trial which is to try you, as though some strange thing happened unto you: But rejoice, inasmuch as ye are partakers of Christ's sufferings; that, when his glory shall be revealed, ye may be glad also with exceeding joy. If ye be reproached for the name of Christ, happy *are ye*; for the spirit of glory and of God resteth upon you: on their part he is evil spoken of, but on your part he is glorified. - **1 Peter 4:12–14 (KJV)**

And ye have forgotten the exhortation which speaketh unto you as unto children, My son, despise not thou the chastening of the Lord, nor faint when thou art rebuked of him: For whom the Lord loveth he chasteneth, and scourgeth every son whom he receiveth. If ye endure chastening, God dealeth with you as with sons; for what son is he whom the father chasteneth not? But if ye be without chastisement, whereof all are partakers, then are ye bastards, and not sons. Furthermore we have had fathers of our flesh which corrected *us*, and we gave *them* reverence: shall we not much rather be in subjection unto the Father of spirits, and live? For they verily for a few days chastened *us* after their own pleasure; but he for *our* profit, that *we* might be partakers of his holiness. Now no chastening for the present seemeth to be joyous, but grievous: nevertheless afterward it yieldeth the peaceable fruit of righteousness unto them which are exercised thereby. - **Hebrews 12:5–11 (KJV)**

These things I have spoken unto you, that in me ye might have peace. In the world ye shall have tribulation: but be of good cheer; I have overcome the world. - **John 16:33 (KJV)**

But he knoweth the way that I take: *when* he hath tried me, I shall come forth as gold. - **Job 23:10 (KJV)**

CHAPTER 6 - EVIL IS IN GOD'S GOOD HANDS

Soldier of Christ, if thou enlisteth, thou wilt have to do hard battle. There is no bed of down for thee; there it no riding to heaven in a chariot; the rough way must be trodden; mountains must be climbed, rivers must be forded, dragons must be fought, giants must be slain, difficulties must be overcome, and great trials must be borne. - **Charles H. Spurgeon**

God is able to bear you through every trial; God is able to bring good out of all evil; God is able to comfort you; God is able either to prevent the trouble, or to make you strong enough to bear it. Nothing can happen to you which will be beyond the power of God; and according to His mighty power He will certainly deliver you... Of what are you afraid? Afraid of the devil? God is stronger than Satan. Afraid of death? God is stronger than death. Afraid of poverty? Christ is stronger than poverty. Afraid of sickness? The power of God will sustain you while suffering from the most terrible disease that can possibly come to your mortal frame. - **Charles H. Spurgeon**

We certainly dread diseases, and want, and exile, and prison, and reproach, and death, because we regard them as evils; but when we understand that they are turned through God's kindness unto helps and aids to our salvation, it is ingratitude to murmur, and not willingly to submit to be thus paternally dealt with. - **John Calvin**

Who among us would wish to be deprived of trials if they are necessary for spiritual advancement? - **Charles H. Spurgeon**

We must learn obedience to God through suffering, and endure suffering so that we may reign with Christ in glory. There can be no glory without suffering; there can be no coming forth as gold unless we've endured the fires in the furnace of affliction (Romans 8:16-17; 2 Timothy 2:12; 1 Peter 4:12-14; 1 Peter 5:10; Isaiah 48:10; Job 23:10; 2 Corinthians 12:7-10). In all our sufferings, patience will have her perfect work, for tribulations worketh patience, and patience worketh hope (James 1:2-4; Romans 5:3-5), and when our hope is made complete at the Lord's appearing, we will be vindicated for all of our sufferings (Romans 8:24-25; Psalm 138:8; Isaiah 64:4; 1 Corinthians 2:9).

> Whatever is our misery, and whatever befalls us, it is something less than hell, which we have escaped by Christ, and all will be made up in heaven. The first sight of God and the first glimpse of everlasting glory will recompense all the sorrows of the present life, and as soon as we step into heaven, all shall be forgotten. - **Thomas Manton**

All evils will be turned to work for our ultimate good (Romans 8:28). After all our strivings with sin, and after all our contentions in this present evil world, we will know God all the more through the fellowship of His sufferings. And as we look back on our lives in the light of eternity, where we have been delivered from all evil, we will praise the Lord and say, "*It is good for me that I have been afflicted; that I might learn thy statutes*" (Psalm 119:71).

> God sometimes writes very bitter things against the best and dearest of his saints and servants, both in outward afflictions and inward disquiet; trouble in body and trouble in mind, that he may humble them, and prove them, and do them good in their latter end. - **Matthew Henry**

OVERCOME EVIL WITH GOOD

Our fight with evil teaches us to war with it, and show we are more than conquerors through Him that loved us (Romans 8:37). Conquering evil does not only consist of what we fight against, but involves proving what is worth fighting for, which is goodness and righteousness. God is honing our spiritual character and virtues not simply by resisting what is evil, but by doing what is good and pleasing to Him (Philippians 2:13; 2 Peter 1:2-8). Throughout Scripture, the Lord continually commands and invites us to overcome evil by doing good and righteousness in the world:

> How God anointed Jesus of Nazareth with the Holy Ghost and with power: who went about doing good, and healing all that were oppressed of the devil; for God was with him. - **Acts 10:38 (KJV)**

> For your obedience is come abroad unto all *men*. I am glad therefore on your behalf: but yet I would have you wise unto that which is good, and simple concerning evil. - **Romans 16:19 (KJV)**

> Be not overcome of evil, but overcome evil with good. - **Romans 12:21 (KJV)**

One of the highest goods we can do is to share the gospel; you may not have silver and gold to offer, or be able to provide someone with food and shelter, but if you give a man the gospel, you will give him what he needs above all else — peace with God and eternal rest for his soul (1 John 3:17; 2 Timothy 4:2; Proverbs 11:30; Luke 23:39-42; 1 Peter 3:15; Psalm 32:1-2).

The peace of God, which passeth all understanding, is a

sacred guard to the soul; it shall keep our hearts and minds by Jesus Christ. The value of peace as keeping the heart and mind is exceeding great. It wards off all sorts of evils, and preserves us unto the day of the Lord's appearing. - **Charles H. Spurgeon**

Beyond the gospel, whether it be for our personal holiness, in our marriages, among our family and friends, in our church and community, on our jobs, and in the public square, God wants us to do good unto all men, and in doing so, we take ground and further overcome the evil in our world (Galatians 6:10; 1 Thessalonians 5:15, 21-22; Psalm 34:14; 1 Corinthians 15:58; 1 Peter 2:11-12; Philippians 2:14-16; 1 Peter 3:8-11, 16; Proverbs 14:19; 2 Corinthians 9:8; Micah 6:8; Romans 12:9).

Evil is in our midst. As long as it's called today, evil in every form is the enemy we must fight, not the ally we embrace. This is what it means to fight the good fight of faith (1 Timothy 6:11-12; 2 Timothy 4:7-8). Christian, overcome evil with good!

If you still don't like the idea of being subjected to evil, and enduring suffering for God's glory, remember how Christ Jesus approached evil and suffering as God Incarnate; no one was subjected to more evil and suffering than Jesus, yet He rendered to the God who created evil a perfect and sinless obedience (Philippians 2:5-11). As eternal debtors to God, we owe Him no less, even with all that evil brings. You don't like how God does things? Obedience or eternal destruction are your only available options. I implore you by the mercies of God to choose wisely (Deuteronomy 30:15-20; Ezekiel 33:11).

EVIL IS IN GOD'S GOOD HANDS

Evil is not good, but it is *for* good (Isaiah 5:20). Evil itself is not a good thing, but evil in God's hands is a good thing, for evil is not left to its own devices to sovereignly operate as it pleases,

CHAPTER 6 - EVIL IS IN GOD'S GOOD HANDS

nor does God have to wrestle and wrangle evil to subject and steer it for His purposes. God created evil, is sovereignly in control of its operations and limitations, and will use evil to serve His preeminent purpose to glorify Himself. God will do the impossible, and bring good out of evil (Job 14:4; Job 12:22; Romans 3:8).

> We believe in a God of purposes and plans. He has not left a blind fate to terrorize the world. - **Charles H. Spurgeon**

As a final point of encouragement, let's talk about a topic that harmonizes the evil of sin and moral wickedness, along with the evil of bad outcomes into one, and show how God can bring good out of evil. This topic is a very sensitive one, and it is heart-wrenching for those who have experienced it. I want us to explore the loss of an infant.

With the evil of sin and moral wickedness, infants commonly die when they are killed by their mothers and fathers in the womb (Exodus 20:13; Genesis 9:6); some parents voluntarily murder their children through the visceral practice of abortion, or voluntarily murder their children through the covert use of birth control in the name of demonic, family planning (sadly, a common practice among Christians these days). Parents sacrifice their babies on the altar of convenience to preserve their comfort and ease (Deuteronomy 27:24-25; Jeremiah 2:34; Leviticus 18:21; Deuteronomy 12:31; Deuteronomy 18:10; Ezekiel 16:20-22).

With the evil of bad outcomes, infants die when they are spontaneously lost during their conception, birth, or their infancy, usually against the desires of their parents. These infant deaths also occurred when God instructed Israel to kill them as a form of righteous judgment (Deuteronomy 32:39-43; 1 Samuel 2:6; Numbers 31:1-17; Joshua 6:20-21; 1 Samuel

15:1-3). Unlike abortion, miscarriages and infant death are involuntary losses (Exodus 21:22-25; Numbers 5:11-31; Job 3:16; Psalm 58:8; Job 10:18-19).

As I mentioned chapters ago, the sovereign God presides over the fate of every child that was ever conceived and born, and every child that was lost in conception, birth, or infancy (Genesis 30:1-2; Exodus 12:29-30; 2 Samuel 12:13-23; Psalm 22:9-10; Psalm 71:5-6; Psalm 127:3; Isaiah 66:9; Jeremiah 1:4-5; Exodus 23:25-26; Ecclesiastes 11:5; Psalm 139:13-16). So whether they were destroyed through the cruelty of abortion, or they were tragically lost in conception, birth or infancy, the LORD is sovereign over the life of each child subject to these circumstances.

In the midst of these evils, God works out His ultimate good, for God saves the souls of all infants. If you didn't know, all infants and young children go to heaven when they die, as the LORD has made them a protected class among the elect; God makes a gracious exception for them, for they have no opportunity to be exposed to or interpret the creation witness, and do not know their right from their left in making a moral decision, so they do not have the mental capacity to receive or reject the gospel (Deuteronomy 1:39; Jonah 4:11; Isaiah 7:14-16).

Therefore, God mercifully imputes His righteousness to them (Romans 5:17; Isaiah 61:10). Babies and young children are vessels of mercy who are saved by God's grace. From before the foundation of the world, the LORD prepared a place for infants and little children in His eternal kingdom (Matthew 19:13-15; Mark 10:13-16; Luke 18:15-17; Revelation 5:9-10; Deuteronomy 24:16; 1 Kings 14:7-13; Matthew 18:1-3, 14).

> God has a tender regard to little children, and is ready to pity and succour them... that though they are not capable

of doing him any service (for they cannot discern between their right hand and their left, between good and evil, sin and duty), yet they are capable of participating in his favours and of obtaining salvation. - **Matthew Henry**

But I rejoice to know that the souls of all infants, as soon as they die, speed their way to paradise. Think what a multitude there is of them! - **Charles H. Spurgeon**

If you want a more comprehensive view on this topic, *Safe in the Arms of God* by John MacArthur is a good read, from what I've heard. When Christ said that the kingdom of heaven is made up of infants and little children, He wasn't kidding, and He wasn't speaking metaphorically — infants and little children are truly in the arms of God, and are forever at rest under His care. The evils of this world did not prevail over these little ones, for the LORD has worked it out for their triumphant good.

The world may revel in their bloodlust of abortion, and have participated in the destruction of millions of helpless image-bearers throughout the ages, but not one of them has been cast aside by God. Christian, you may have murdered your own children through abortion or birth control (chemical abortion), and you may grieve over the guilt of these actions. But what you meant for evil, God meant for good (Genesis 50:20). That which you tore asunder you will bear up in your arms again. Those children you condemned to die have been vindicated with eternal life, and by the grace of God, you will see them again. The evil and wickedness of men is thwarted by the goodness of God.

Christian, you may not have killed your child, but you may have been stricken by the evil of bad outcomes; time and time again, you have lost your precious baby in conception, birth or infancy. Whether it be through the affliction of infertility, or some other ailment or tragedy, the grief you faced from these losses will be turned into joy, for every miscarriage and loss of your child here on earth is an eternal soul gained in heaven. In your earthly losses, the LORD has wrought something of eternal value through you. As you grieve and weep for your children, be comforted and remember that these untimely exits have led to their glorious entrance into God's kingdom. God's final outcome with your children will infinitely surpass all the bad outcomes. As an added bonus, look up "fetal microchimerism", and tell me whether God is not the God of all comfort, who brings consolation in this particular tribulation:

> Blessed *be* God, even the Father of our Lord Jesus Christ, the Father of mercies, <u>and the God of all comfort; Who comforteth us in all our tribulation, that we may be able to comfort them which are in any trouble, by the comfort wherewith we ourselves are comforted of God. For as the sufferings of Christ abound in us, so our consolation also aboundeth by Christ... And our hope of you *is* stedfast, knowing, that as ye are partakers of the sufferings, so *shall ye be* also of the consolation.</u> - **2 Corinthians 1:3-5, 7 (KJV)**

This is just *one* example of God bringing good out of evil. There is nowhere that evil abounds that God's goodness will not much more abound. Take heart, believer. God will make all things right in the end. Let us occupy ourselves with welldoing until He comes (Luke 19:13). To the praise and glory of His name, the LORD will do valiantly in triumphing over all evil (Psalm 60:12). Evil is in good hands — in God's good hands.

> Patience, then, believer, eternity will right the wrongs of time. - **Charles H. Spurgeon**

Beloved, believe not every spirit, but try the spirits whether they are of God: because many false prophets are gone out into the world.

1 JOHN 4:1 (KJV)

The study of God's word reveals
The way to our eternal King;
Whose hand created heav'n and earth,
And of Whose pow'r we tell and sing;
Each precious promise fills the heart
With inspirations from above,
Awakening hopes and holy thoughts
Of that bright land where all is love.

The study of God's word invites
The weary, wand'ring, doubting one
To follow God in that new life,
Procured for us through His dear Son;
It tells of grace and "Love divine,"
Of endless blessings rich and free,
Of living streams and pastures green,
Where Jesus reigns eternally.

The study of God's word imparts
A comfort and a restful peace;
A shining light that leads the way
To joys that nevermore shall cease;
A lasting strength that never fails,
When we approach the coming foe;
A Rock, on which our feet can stand,
In every conflict here below.

The study of God's word foretells
The glory of that golden shore,
Where "Heav'nly hosts" in triumph sing
And praise their King forevermore.
It warns us of the wrath to come
For those who never seek their Lord,
It bids us trust in God alone,
"And take Him at His promised word."

Lavinia E. Brauff

EPILOGUE
The Stress Test for Sound Doctrine

> Beloved, believe not every spirit, but try the spirits whether they are of God: because many false prophets are gone out into the world.
> **1 John 4:1 (KJV)**

Outside of the Bible, I feel this will probably be the most controversial book you will ever read, for it may speak to the most controversial topic Christians have ever heard. Proverbs 22:3 and Proverbs 27:12 say, "A prudent *man* foreseeth the evil, and hideth himself: but the simple pass on, and are punished." God repeated this proverb twice to emphasize its importance. The prudent man is a wise and proactive person. His wisdom allows him to understand what's happening, and foresee future outcomes in the present. His prudence allows him to take stock of any looming evil and danger, which gives him time to avoid or guard against the evil when it comes.

I would be simple-minded and naïve if I didn't apply foresight to the potential reception of this book. While some readers may receive the content of this book with joy, there may be others who will use this book to attack my character, and critique my intentions. Some Christians might label me as a false prophet who is corrupting the Word of God, teaching doctrines of devils, and seeking to make merchandise of the Church for my financial gain (2 Corinthians 2:17; 1 Timothy 4:1; 2 Peter 2:1-3; Ephesians 4:14; Titus 1:10-14).

Knowing these allegations may arise, I want to properly address them. First and foremost, let's get these false prophet accusations out of the way. I wrote this book to glorify God first, but I also wrote this book to exercise my God-given giftings and skills, and create something of value that could be monetized in the marketplace. There is nothing wrong with this, as our gifts make room for us, and can be the means through which God allows us to get wealth (Proverbs 18:16; Proverbs 24:27; Deuteronomy 8:18).

In Deuteronomy 25, God instructed Israel to not "muzzle the ox when he treadeth out *the corn*" (Deuteronomy 25:4). The New Testament Church extracted the underlying principle from this command, and applied it to properly compensating workers for their labour, namely those who laboured for the sake of the gospel (1 Corinthians 9:1-14; 1 Timothy 5:17-18). A worker who serves another should be compensated for their work, and should not be deprived of what they need to work effectively. No worker should be deprived of what they are entitled to.

This book was the product of a lot of time, energy and study, and therefore, I will not be ashamed in seeking to be recompensed for my labour. Ecclesiastes 9:10 tells us to work with all our might (working diligently with all our physical and mental energies); 1 Corinthians 10:31 emphasizes that whatever we do should be for God's glory, and Colossians 3:23 implores us to work as if God was our boss. As long as my biblical priorities are in order, any skill that can be monetized is valuable work, and if it's not rooted in covetousness or vainglory, seeking financial gain through these skills is a reasonable expectation. I think many authors would agree this — even with God's glory being prioritized, many write with the prospect of making money in their minds, and that is truly okay. It is an earnest way to make a living, if God permits.

EPILOGUE - THE STRESS TEST FOR SOUND DOCTRINE

I want this book to do well in the way that God *intends* for it to do well. I don't know what the future holds, but I'm stepping out on faith, and entrusting God with the results (Hebrews 11:6; 2 Corinthians 5:7; Romans 14:23). I may never sell one copy. I may sell millions of copies. Whatever my lot, I leave it in God's hands.

I hope this book does well commercially, as I laboured with the hope that it sells, but I pray that even if I sold 100 copies, and it edified every single reader of those copies, I would rejoice in God for producing that fruit. I want this book to do well, but not at the cost of shipwrecking the faith of young believers. The LORD provides a strong warning of causing spiritual babes in the faith to stumble (Matthew 18:6; Mark 9:42), and I receive that warning with fear and trembling. It is not a light thing to expound upon Scripture, and it is a fearful thing to fall into the hands of God (James 3:1; Hebrews 10:31).

As I said earlier, this book is for an intended group. If the Spirit of God is guiding you into all truth, and this truth is what you've been earnestly looking for, then this book is for you. I pray this book will never reach the ears of those who are not intended to hear it, and I pray this book will never reach the eyes of those who are not intended to see it. That is why I issued the warnings I did in Chapter 1, and disqualified a large segment of prospective readers at my own expense.

My desire is to protect the vulnerable and unlearned from weighty doctrine, not brazenly invite them to partake in something they are not ready to handle, plunging them into theological confusion just to make a quick dollar. My aim in writing this book is for the glory of God, and for the edifying of the saints in Jesus Christ (Ephesians 4:11-16).

Secondly, for those who contend that I am spewing false doctrine or the doctrines of devils, I humbly invite you to put my doctrine to the test. In fact, *God* invites you to put my doctrine to the test, for you shouldn't blindly accept what I've written as true. Regardless of how well I've presented my arguments, none of it should be received as truth until it has been fact-checked, scrutinized, and confirmed by the Word of God. Without the full support of Scripture, what I claim as theology is simply vain philosophy.

> The Word of God is the anvil upon which the opinions of men are smashed. - **Charles H. Spurgeon (attributed quote)**

The Bible is the stress test for all doctrine, and only sound doctrine can stand under its weight. All false doctrine will crumble under the pressure of God's divine truth. Therefore, Scripture must be the immovable standard by which we filter all truth.

A good example of a biblical stress test can be found in Acts 17. In the first century AD, the Apostle Paul was someone who many considered to be a biblical scholar. He was well-trained in the affairs of the Mosaic law and Judaic traditions as Saul, but as Paul — through the Holy Spirit — he wrote many dissertations (epistles) discussing theology, Christology, pneumatology, anthropology, hamartiology, soteriology, ecclesiology, eschatology, chronology and sociology. When it came to matters involving Christ, the gospel, and biblical history, Paul had a PhD equivalent and more.

At this point in Acts, this is Paul's second missionary journey. He, along with Silas and Timothy (Timotheus) have travelled through many cities preaching the gospel, and have now arrived at Berea to minister (Acts 17:10-14). This is what God had to say about the Bereans who heard Paul's preaching:

> These were more noble than those in Thessalonica, in that

they received the word with all readiness of mind, and searched the scriptures daily, whether those things were so. Therefore many of them believed; also of honourable women which were Greeks, and of men, not a few. - **Acts 17:11-12 (KJV)**

The Bereans were willing to accept the truth from those who came in the name of the Lord, but since the gospel of Jesus Christ was a new concept to them, they needed a point of reference, and their reference was God's Word (the Scriptures). They looked to God's written Word to discern and confirm what was true. Searching the Scriptures daily infers that they were diligent and dedicated to the truth. They were counted as more noble because they scrutinized the information being presented to them with the Scriptures. This was a practical example of "trying the spirits" that the Apostle John referenced in 1 John:

Beloved, believe not every spirit, but try the spirits whether they are of God: because many false prophets are gone out into the world. - **1 John 4:1 (KJV)**

The "spirits" used here is not just about spiritual beings, but spirits include thoughts, perspectives, ideologies, professions, belief systems, paradigms, ways of life, and narratives that are presented to us as truth. We "try the spirits" by looking to see if any of these things properly align with the Bible.

Paul could have claimed he was an expert. He could have claimed that he was sent by God as an apostle. Paul could have tried to hinder the Bereans from searching for themselves, or be offended that they did not blindly trust what he said. For Paul was only reiterating what God had already said, and what was now His commission to Paul — preaching the gospel to the

Gentiles. Regardless, the Bereans would fact-check him; it didn't matter what kind of expertise Paul had, or what apostolic authority he was under — if it didn't line up with God's Word, they weren't buying it. Claiming to be a spiritual expert would not get you far among the Bereans.

For them, trusting a supposed expert would have been foolish if it meant disregarding what God had written. Their scrutiny by leaning on God's Word ultimately led to a blessing, as many of the Bereans became Christians and believed the gospel. God's Word allows us to discern the *completely* true from the *almost* true (a lie).

In our assessments, we should educate ourselves to gain an understanding (Proverbs 1:5; Proverbs 9:9); we should cross-examine the evidence (Proverbs 18:17); we should dig deep to see all matters through the lens of Scripture (Proverbs 25:2; 2 Timothy 2:15); and discern and confirm what the perfect will of God is (Romans 12:2; Hebrews 4:12-13). When we do this, we will effectively apply the biblical stress test, and can make clear-cut distinctions between false and sound doctrine.

I don't have a monopoly on the truth. But God does! So if we are instructed to try the spirits, then we are instructed to test every thought, every perspective, every ideology, every profession, every belief system, every paradigm, every way of life, and every narrative against God's Word. This way, we can see if there is any merit or any truth in those things according to what God has said. The Bible is pure truth (Psalm 19:9). Truth shouldn't take offence to scrutiny because it knows what it is! Truth is not afraid of being questioned, but lies despise being challenged. Therefore, I invite biblical scrutiny because the doctrine I've presented is able to stand up under it, by God's grace.

If you're going to be Berean about it, you need to bring your King James Bible and a ready mind. This book will force you to look at God's written Word, and search the Scriptures for yourself. Conduct your own extensive Bible study, check every Scripture reference I've made in this book, and see for yourself whether these things are so. Pray that God will open your understanding (Luke 24:44-49), and open your eyes to see the beautiful truths of Scripture (Psalm 119:18). It is truth that will radically transform and empower you (Psalm 19:7-11).

> Study the Bible with diligence. Never be satisfied with a secondhand version of it. - **Charles H. Spurgeon (attributed quote)**

> The more truth you believe, the more sanctified you will be. - **Charles H. Spurgeon**

Another thing we can learn from the Bereans' encounter with Paul is just because a doctrine is theologically new to you, doesn't mean it is blasphemous (Hosea 8:12). None of us Christians are the perfect sum of wisdom and knowledge; we don't have a perfect knowledge of all theology at any point in our lives. The doctrine of illumination by the Holy Spirit reinforces this (John 14:26; John 16:13; 1 Corinthians 2:6-16; 1 John 2:27; Colossians 1:9-12; Ephesians 1:17-18; Ephesians 3:14-19; 2 Corinthians 3:12-18; 2 Corinthians 4:3-6; Hebrews 10:15-16; 1 John 5:20). We are all students continually sitting at the feet of the Master as we are guided into all truth, and taught all things through the Holy Spirit at work in us.

> Nobody ever outgrows Scripture; the book widens and deepens with our years. - **Charles H. Spurgeon**

We don't know everything about God as soon as we are regenerated. We are introduced to new concepts, gain a deeper understanding of old concepts, and continue to grow in our theology as we mine the riches of God's inexhaustible Word. There are aspects of theology we've learned today that we could have never received or accepted 5 years prior, or 10 years prior. Just because something is theologically new to you, doesn't mean it's blasphemous — it's just new, especially if it's unequivocally supported by Scripture.

> The canon of revelation is closed; there is no more to be added; God does not give a fresh revelation, but He rivets the old one. When it has been forgotten, and laid in the dusty closet of our memory, He grabs it out and cleans the picture, but does not paint a new one. There are no new doctrines, but the old ones are often revived. It is not, I say, by any new revelation that the Holy Spirit comforts. He does so by telling us old things over and over again; He brings a bright light to manifest the treasures hidden in Scripture; He unlocks the vaults in which the truth has long lain, and He points to secret rooms filled with untold riches; but He coins no more, for enough is done. Believer! There is enough in the Bible for you to live on forever. - **Charles H. Spurgeon**

I really love the analogy Spurgeon uses for Scripture in the quote above. There is no fresh revelation outside of the canon of Scripture; I'm not revealing some newfangled doctrine which never existed in the Bible in the first place. This doctrine was already there. However, by rejecting Isaiah 45:7, we missed out on accessing the treasures and riches already hidden deep within Scripture.

These truths have long been there, but we were unwilling to search for them. Isaiah 45:7 was the key to access the vaults, and enter into the secret rooms of Scripture where few

Christians have ventured into. Up until this book, with all the truth currently available to us, in my eyes, no Christian had provided a full biblical answer for evil's origin, evil's purpose, and God's relationship to evil. No one was properly putting the pieces together, and trust me, I did my research; I scoured the Internet for blogs, videos and sermons of different pastors and theologians on this topic, but all the answers available on evil's origin were obscure and inconclusive.

As a result, I decided toss my hat into the theological ring, and provide some biblical clarity through this book (Job 32:1-20; Psalm 119:97-100). There are secrets in Scripture that God has laid out for us to find, but we have to search them out by searching the Scriptures (John 5:39), and that is what this book was intended to do:

> The secret *things belong* unto the LORD our God: but those *things which are* revealed *belong* unto us and to our children for ever, that *we* may do all the words of this law. - **Deuteronomy 29:29 (KJV)**

Check the Fruits of My Labour

In addition to trying the spirits, you must apply the principle of fruit examination to discern sound doctrine. This is important to explore, for Jesus Christ said, "every tree is known by his own fruit..." (Luke 6:44). If you want to mature in godly discernment, you must grasp this principle.

One of the most powerful ways you can examine the virtue of a thing is to examine the fruit it produces. The fruit produced tells you a lot about the nature of the tree from which it grows. The "tree" can be a person, a group, an organization, a product, an invention or an idea.

Whatever the tree is, you can discern the good or evil character of that tree according to the fruit it bears. If it bears biblically good fruit, it is most likely a good tree. If it bears biblically evil fruit, it is most likely an evil tree. It is not the *only* way to examine and discern biblical virtue, but it is a prudent and powerful method. When Jesus introduced this principle, He was specifically referencing how to discern a person's spiritual condition (Luke 6:43-45; Matthew 7:15-20). Despite the context, the principle of fruit examination can be applied to almost anything.

Has this book produced any good fruit in you? Have you gained a clearer spiritual perspective through studying biblical theology? Do you see the beauty of God's grace in full view? Are you now in greater awe of God and His Word? Has your exploration of evil spurred you to war against sin, and contend with evil for God's glory? If your answer to all these questions is "yes", then it is highly likely that this book is good fruit from a good tree, and is deserving of your attention and meditations:

> Finally, brethren, whatsoever things are true, whatsoever things *are* honest, whatsoever things *are* just, whatsoever things *are* pure, whatsoever things *are* lovely, whatsoever things *are* of good report; <u>if *there be* any virtue, and if *there be* any praise, think on these things.</u> Those things, which ye have both learned, and received, and heard, and seen in me, do: and the God of peace shall be with you. - **Philippians 4:8-9 (KJV)**

As I stated chapters ago, I pray that this book will bless and enrich the life of every Christian who reads it. I hope this book edified you in a remarkable way.

Good books enrich; bad books bewitch. - **Charles H. Spurgeon**

EPILOGUE - THE STRESS TEST FOR SOUND DOCTRINE

Did Not Our Hearts Burn Within Us?

Outside of the biblical stress test and the principle of fruit examination, if you're a Christian, you will gravitate to and resonate with sound doctrine, and I want to end this book with a story from Scripture to illustrate this.

This beautiful account is found in Luke 24. We find ourselves among two disciples, who are journeying from Jerusalem to a village called Emmaus. It is the first day of the week, and the third day when Jesus said He would rise after being crucified. The Lord has risen indeed, but these disciples have yet to see Him. Suspecting that their hope in the risen Lord may not be real, the two disciples are saddened by the circumstances, and are discussing all the things which occurred because of Jesus (Luke 24:13-14). Unbeknownst to them, Jesus appears and joins them on their journey:

> And it came to pass, that, while they communed *together* and reasoned, Jesus himself drew near, and went with them. But their eyes were holden that they should not know him. And he said unto them, What manner of communications *are* these that ye have one to another, as ye walk, and are sad? - **Luke 24:15-17 (KJV)**

Assuming He was a foreigner, the two disciples inform Jesus about Jesus of Nazareth, including His crucifixion and promised resurrection (Luke 24:18-24). The stranger Jesus begins to rebuke the disciples for their unbelief, but He does not leave them there. Christ goes one step further:

> Then he said unto them, O fools, and slow of heart to believe all that the prophets have spoken: Ought not Christ to have suffered these things, and to enter into his glory? And beginning at Moses and all the prophets, he

expounded unto them in all the scriptures the things concerning himself. - Luke 24:25-27 (KJV)

Jesus transforms this mundane walk into one of the greatest, Bible studies ever recorded in human history. Jesus takes these disciples on a journey throughout the entire Old Testament, for "Moses" (the law) and the prophets (Elijah/Elias) were used as placeholders to represent the entire body of Old Testament Scripture (Matthew 5:17; Matthew 17:1-9; Matthew 22:34-40; Luke 16:27-31; John 1:45). Christ begins to expound and unfold the deep mysteries of the Old Testament, and shows how all the Scriptures testified of Him (John 5:39), particularly His life, death, burial and resurrection. Jesus does something similar to this with His core, eleven disciples later in the chapter (Luke 24:44-49). All of this is going on, yet the two disciples still think He is a stranger.

Once they reach Emmaus, the two disciples compel Christ to abide with them for the night, which extends their time of fellowship, and gives them an opportunity to share a meal with their new friend. As Christ breaks the bread for the meal, the two disciples finally realize that this man is no stranger, but the risen Lord Himself! Upon this realization, Christ suddenly vanishes out of their sight (Luke 24:28-31). Hear what these disciples say and do after this surprising encounter:

And they said one to another, Did not our heart burn within us, while he talked with us by the way, and while he opened to us the scriptures? And they rose up the same hour, and returned to Jerusalem, and found the eleven gathered together, and them that were with them, Saying, The Lord is risen indeed, and hath appeared to Simon. And they told what things *were done* in the way, and how he was known of them in breaking of bread. And as they thus spake, Jesus himself stood in the midst of them, and saith unto them, Peace *be* unto you. - **Luke 24:32–36 (KJV)**

What's the point of this story? Well, let's first look at Christ. Jesus loved His disciples (John 10:11-18; John 11:5; John 13:34-35; John 14:15-21; John 15:9-14; John 17). He appeared to His disciples not just to confirm His bodily resurrection, but to comfort them, and turn their sorrows into joy (John 16:16-22). This is clearly what happened with the two disciples; they left Jerusalem in sorrow, but returned to Jerusalem with joy.

In His love, Christ devoted Himself to walk and commune with them, to teach them the Scriptures, and abide with them. In the end, Christ left them with their hearts burning. To have their "heart burn within" them implies that Jesus kindled their zeal. He gave them a spiritual fervour to do good. Their zeal led them to be a testimony of the resurrected Christ, for they rushed back to Jerusalem to tell the eleven, who were in hiding because they were afraid (John 20:19).

I hope this book will do the same thing. I hope to be like Jesus in this way. I hope my words will cause your heart to stir because of the truth, bring you from despair to joy, and fill your mouths with truth to encourage others. Christian, I hope this book blessed you, and if this book is of great edification to the Church, may the LORD receive all the glory, for I was marvellously helped (2 Chronicles 26:15). May God be glorified through this book, world without end (Psalm 50:23). Amen.

It is a great refreshment to a good man to have liberty to speak for the glory of God and the edification of others. - **Matthew Henry**

And the Lord shall deliver me from every evil work, and will preserve *me* unto his heavenly kingdom: to whom *be* glory for ever and ever. Amen.

2 TIMOTHY 4:18 (KJV)

BIBLIOGRAPHY

Sproul, R. C. (2021, May 12). *Does Prayer Change God's Mind?* Ligonier Ministries. https://www.ligonier.org/learn/articles/does-prayer-change-gods-mind

IF THIS BOOK HAS BEEN A BLESSING TO YOU, PLEASE LEAVE US A REVIEW.

www.ingramcontent.com/pod-product-compliance
Lightning Source LLC
Chambersburg PA
CBHW030548080526
44585CB00012B/301